Celebrate! IV

THE ANNUAL FOR CAKE DECORATORS

EDITED BY EUGENE T. AND MARILYNN C. SULLIVAN

WILTON ENTERPRISES, INC.,
WOODRIDGE, ILLINOIS

Celebrate! IV

DECORATING CONSULTANT: Norman Wilton

CO-EDITORS:
Marilynn C. Sullivan
and Eugene T. Sullivan

DECORATORS:
Michael Nitzsche, Senior decorator
Amy Rohr, John Walter, Hoa Dong

CONTRIBUTING DECORATORS:
Larry Olkiewicz, Guadalupe
DeDomani, Luz DeHoyos,
Laura Goodman

ART ASSISTANTS:
Sandra Larson, Carol Zaleski

EDITORIAL ASSISTANT: Melissa Jess

PRODUCTION ASSISTANT: Ethel LaRoche

READERS' EDITOR: Diane Kish

STAFF PHOTOGRAPHER: Edward Hois

Editorial mail should be addressed to:
  Wilton Book Division
  1603 South Michigan Avenue
  Chicago, Illinois 60616
Photographs and other material submitted for
publication must be accompanied by a stamped,
self-addressed envelope, if return is requested.

CELEBRATE!® IV
THE ANNUAL FOR CAKE DECORATORS
is published by Wilton Enterprises, Inc.
Vincent A. Naccarato, President

Library of Congress Catalog Card Number: 75-24148
International Standard Book Number: 0-912696-10-9

Celebrate! IV

Dear Friends,

Love is the theme of *Celebrate! IV*. The love of the art-form that you practice. The love for the person for whom you decorate a beautiful cake. The love that is given back when that person responds with delight to the beauty you have created. Just see the smiles!

Love is what decorating is about.

Preparing this book for you has truly been a labor of love. You have helped us immeasurably by your advice and suggestions. A sincere thank you to all who have taken the time to write.

All of us on the Book Division staff hope that *Celebrate! IV* will give you many years of pleasure. I would appreciate your comments—write to me at the Book Division address, 1603 South Michigan Avenue, Chicago, Illinois 60616.

We have prepared a companion book, *The Celebrate! IV Pattern Book*, which contains all the patterns needed for *Celebrate! IV*.

Sincerely,

NORMAN WILTON

Celebrate!®

JANUARY/FEBRUARY...
put a little love in your life

Decorating directions
on page 22

Happy New Year

Put a little love in your life

AND SOMEONE ELSE'S TOO

Use your skill and artistry to express your love to someone dear—and have fun doing it! Lavish a cake with roses, blushing hearts, ruffles and swirls. Here are cakes for valentine's day, shower cakes, love's announcement cakes and splendid cakes to wish happiness in the new year. Some are simple, others challenging, all will bring pleasure to those for whom you made them. We've included a mini-decorating course so you can introduce a young friend to this fascinating art—or use it to brush up your own skills. Happy days, happy New Year!

Bake a rosy valentine

This stunning old-fashioned cake with a three-dimensional look can be adapted for many occasions. It's a valentine's day cake, an engagement cake, a cake for a bridal shower or to just say "I love you."

1. Roll out gum paste ⅛" thick (recipe on page 22) and cut a heart from Celebrate! IV pattern. Dry, then pipe message with tube 2. Add tube 3 beading around edge of heart.

2. Pipe two roses and one bud. Pipe a tube 10 ball of icing on a piece of heavy florists' wire. Dry. Pipe petals with tube 104, making center petals slightly darker than outer ones. Pipe sepals with tube 65s. Make many tube 101s forget-me-nots with tube 1s centers. Pipe tube 67 leaves on wires. Dry all thoroughly.

3. Bake a 9" x 4" heart cake. Fill and ice with buttercream, and place on serving tray. Pipe tube 16 bottom shell border. On side of cake, about 1" up from bottom, drop a row of tube 2 strings as a guideline. Pipe tube 104 ruffles over strings and edge top of ruffles with tube 3 beading. About 1" down from top of cake, drop a triple row of tube 3 strings, lining up with ruffles. Top intersections with a tube 3 curl of icing.

4. Pipe tube 14 top shell border. On top of cake, pipe tube 104 scallops, using side strings as a guide. Pipe a tube 14 star at intersections. Position flowers and heart as shown, securing with icing. Add a ribbon bow. Serves twelve.

Give someone your heart

Top a Valentine cake with a sweet ornament you made yourself from brilliant icing carnations.

1. Make carnations. Using tube 103 and stiff icing for broken edge on petals, move out about 1⅛", jiggling tube gently and lifting slightly as you reach petal tip. Curve around, return to center and stop pressure. Make a full circle of petals in this manner, then do two more rows, making each shorter. Fill center with upright petals. Make more carnations with tube 104. You will need 14 of each size. Dry.

2. Make gum paste following the instructions on page 22. Using Celebrate! IV patterns, cut out one ⅛" thick solid heart, one ¼" thick open heart and 25 thin small hearts. Dry all pieces flat.

Pipe message on large solid heart with tube 2. Then trim edge with tube 3 loops and dots. Attach pieces of fine florists' wire to backs of small hearts with egg white. Dry.

3. Make top ornament. Twist heavy florists' wire into a "Y" shape and "glue" to back of open heart with egg white. Brush entire back of heart with egg white and cut second open heart. Attach while wet over wire, back to back against dried heart to form framework for carnations. Dry. Cover wire at bottom of heart with floral tape. Attach carnations to framework with dots of royal icing. Attach Winged Angel to carnation at inside point of heart window with a dot of icing.

4. Bake a two-layer 10" square cake. Fill and ice with buttercream. Place on a foil-covered cake board, edged with Tuk-N-Ruffle. Pipe tube 7 bottom bulb border. Using patterns, mark hearts at corners and on top of cake. Pipe tube 4 top bulb border between hearts.

Pipe tube 2 cornelli lace on top of cake, leaving heart in center plain. Pipe tube 3 loops and dots within edges of hearts on top and corners, then edge with tube 3 beading.

5. Attach solid heart to side of cake with icing. Pipe a mound of icing at each corner of cake on the Tuk-N-Ruffle and insert wires of small hearts. Attach carnations around them with more icing. Insert wire of heart window into center of heart on top·of cake. The result is a beautiful love cake to serve 20.

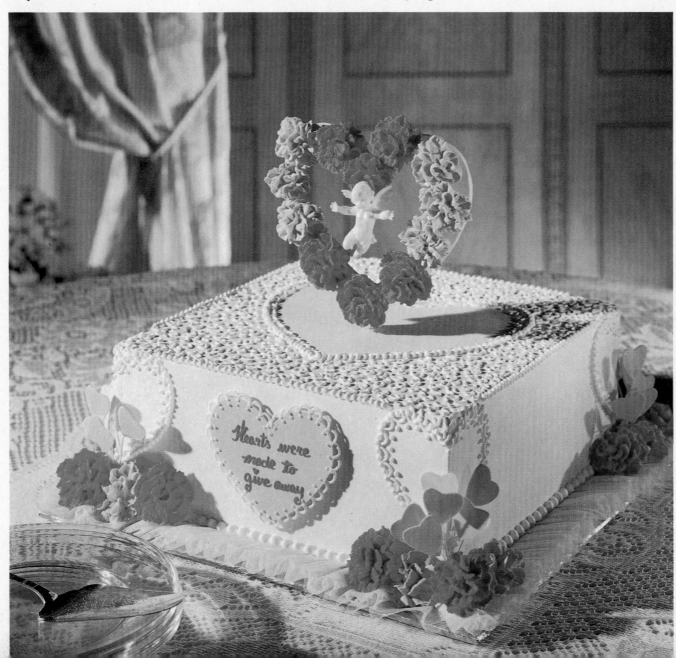

Pipe a jolly pair of lovers

The adorable little people on top of this cake are figure piped. They're quick to do, and add a whimsical touch to a Valentine love cake.

1. Pipe the figures with royal icing. On a piece of wax paper, pipe tube 2A head and add tube 8 neck. Pipe tube 3 nose and tube 2 eyes and mouth. Pipe tube 8 hands with tube 3 thumbs. Make tube 32 feet and hats. Dry.

Make body on wax paper with tube 4B. Pipe arms and legs with tube 32. Add tube 14 ruffles and attach feet, hands and head. Pipe tube 2 hair and attach hat. Add a tube 3 heart-shaped button on front of girl figure. Dry.

2. Bake 10″ x 4″ square and 9″ x 2″ heart tiers. Ice and assemble on foil-covered board. Divide each side of square tier into fourths. On front of cake between the two outer divisions pipe tube 1 message. Pipe a vertical tube 17 line at remaining divisions around cake. Drop two tube 13 scallops from point to point at top edge of cake. Pipe a tube 16 puff between vertical lines at bottom border, then circle entire base of cake with tube 16 stars. Make 18 tube 32 hearts on wax paper and dry.

Pipe tube 17 bottom shell border around heart tier. Pipe tube 16 "C" shapes around top edge. Add a tube 16 star between them.

3. Attach piped hearts. Secure with icing along top edge at vertical lines. Secure figures to cake with icing. Serves 26.

Jewel a frothy cake

This elegant cake is adorned with sparkling candy hearts and fluffy icing scrolls. It looks impressive but is quick to do.

1. Make 16 small hearts in hard candy molds and one large heart in heart cupcake pan using recipe below. Oil the molds well—use one teaspoon of oil in the cupcake pan.

HARD CANDY RECIPE

   2 cups granulated sugar
   ⅔ cup water
   ¼ teaspoon cream of tartar
   Food coloring
   1 teaspoon Hard Candy Flavor

Combine water, sugar and cream of tartar in saucepan and bring to boil over high heat, stirring constantly. Stir in coloring, insert candy thermometer and stop stirring. Brush sides of pan occasionally with a wet pastry brush. When temperature

reaches 280°F, turn to low heat and add flavoring. Cook until temperature reaches 300°F, remove from heat and pour into oiled molds.

2. Bake a 10″ x 4″ square, two-layer cake. Fill, ice and place on cake board. Transfer heart patterns to sides and top of cake. Pipe tube 17 bottom shell border. Attach small candy hearts to cake sides and pipe tube 2 beading around them. Pipe tube 14 "C" shapes to define heart shapes and add fleurs-de-lis and rosettes.

3. Attach large candy heart in center of cake and surround with tube 3 beading. Pipe tube 15 "C" shapes to define heart shapes. Add fleurs-de-lis and rosettes with the same tube. Pipe tube 14 top shell border. Trim cake board with ¼″ ribbon and attach a small bow. Serves 20.

Circle a cake with hearts

This stunning Victorian-style valentine shows how side trim can enhance a cake.

1. Make drop flowers with tubes 131 and 225. Add tube 2 centers. Dry.

2. Assemble ornament using a Cherub from the Musical Trio, the small Filigree Heart and the top plate from the petite Heart Base. Glue together and dry. Paint heart and base with thinned royal icing. Dry, then pipe tube 2 hearts and scallops on base. Secure drop flowers and add tube 65 leaves.

3. Bake a two-layer 10″ round tier and a 6″ x 2″ heart tier. Ice and assemble on a foil-covered board. Transfer Celebrate! IV patterns to side of 10″ tier. Pipe stylized flowers and heart designs using tubes 2 and 4. Pressure control is very important. Add tube 4 beading around bottom of 10″ tier.

4. Pipe message and beading around top of 10″ tier with tube 2. Make stylized flowers and leaves around heart tier. Pipe tube 4 beading around base of tier, tube 2 beading around top. Attach ornament. Serves 18.

Put a little love in your life

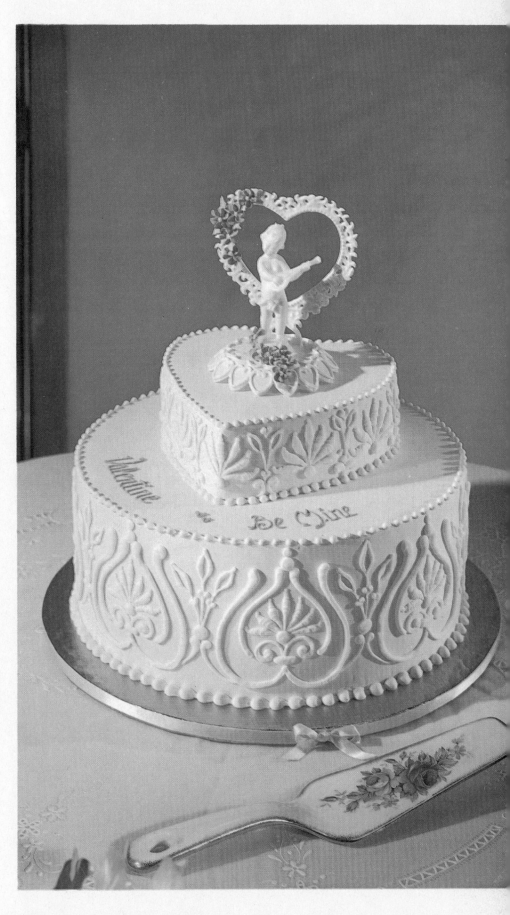

Create love's centerpiece

Announce an engagement, celebrate an anniversary or dress up a bridal shower table with this impressive centerpiece love cake. It's a stunning cake for valentine's day too and simple to make using large tubes, a pattern press and an elegant ornament for between the tiers.

1. Make roses using tubes 104 and 124. Pipe buds and partially opened roses with tube 104. Dry.

2. Bake 6" x 3" and 10" x 4" round, two-layer tiers. Fill, ice and assemble on serving tray using Angelic Serenade separator plates. Pipe tube 16 scallops around bottom separator plate. Pipe tube 2 vines on vase and plate and attach rosebuds and partially opened roses with dots of royal icing so they appear to be climbing and twining up the vase. Pipe sepals on the flowers with tube 2. Add tube 65 leaves.

3. On 10" tier, pipe tube 21 reverse shell base border. Using heart-shaped pattern press, mark eight heart shapes around side of tier. Pipe the design with tube 16 scrolls and add elongated shells and scrolls between them with same tube. Figure pipe a small heart with tube 5 in each heart-shaped design between the upper scrolls.

Attach large roses to base of cake between the heart designs with dots of icing. Secure smaller roses on either side of large roses.

4. Pipe tube 17 reverse shell border around base of 6" tier. Pipe four tube 5 figure piped hearts around side of tier. Write the names of the happy couple with tube 2. Using the pattern press used on the lower tier as a guide, pipe half the heart design on either side of the names with tube 16 scrolls. Pipe a tube 16 reverse shell border around top of 6" tier.

Make a mound of icing on the top of 6" tier and attach roses, partially opened roses and buds to it. Add tube 68 leaves. This love cake serves 20.

Put a little love in your life

Tell love's story

Draped with ruffles and adorned with delicate drop flowers, this cake is a beautiful way to express your own fond feelings.

1. Make tube 225 drop flowers in pink and red. Add tube 2 yellow centers. Dry thoroughly.

2. Bake a 9" x 2" heart tier in the pair of one-mix heart pans (for rounded top) and a 12" x 2" heart tier. Ice and assemble on heart-shaped cake board covered with foil.

3. Pipe a tube 6 bottom bulb border around the base of the 12" tier. Divide each half of the heart into eighths along the side and mark the divisions halfway up the side of the tier. Drop a tube 2 string from point to point as a guideline. Then pipe a tube 104 ruffle garland, following the guide. Add tube 2 beading along the top edge of the ruffle. Attach a pink drop flower at each division with a dot of icing.

4. On the top tier, write "Love" with piping gel and tube 1. Make a heart shape of tube 2 dots about 1" in from the edge of the tier. Attach red and pink drop flowers with dots of icing along the top curves and bottom point of the heart.

5. Pipe a large tube 2A line of icing around the base of the top tier to support ruffle. Pipe a tube 127D large ruffle around the tier, attaching it about ½" below the top of the tier so it just rests on the bottom tier. Bead the top of the ruffle with tube 4. Serves 24.

Let everyone know

Announce an engagement or dress up a bridal shower table with this easy-to-make cake.

1. Make royal icing star-method dove plaque by taping *Celebrate! IV* pattern to a flat surface. Tape a piece of wax paper over it. Outline design with tube 2. Fill in doves with tube 16 stars, heart and background with tube 14 stars. Be sure to pipe the stars very close together. Pipe tube 2 eyes and flatten with a wet fingertip. Pipe tube 16 zigzag around outside of circle. Dry thoroughly, then peel off wax paper.

2. Bake a 10″ x 4″ round, two-layer cake. Fill, ice and place on serving tray. Pipe tube 16 bottom shell border. Divide side of cake into eighths about one-third of the way up the side. Drop a tube 2 guideline from point to point. Following the guideline, pipe a tube 104 ruffle. Add a tube 16 zigzag above and slightly covering the ruffle. Follow guideline when making zigzag.

3. Position royal icing dove plaque in center of cake, attaching with dots of icing. Pipe a tube 103 ruffle around it. Print names with tube 2. Figure pipe a tube 8 heart between them and flatten it with a wet fingertip. Finally, pipe a tube 16 top shell border. Serves 14.

Love-shaped confections

Serve these delicate heart-shaped cupcakes at a bridal shower. They'll make a lovely centerpiece.

1. Pipe tube 103 royal icing roses with deep and light pink icing. Dry.

2. Bake cupcakes in heart cupcake pans. One cake mix makes 18. Ice with a light coat of buttercream icing. Place the cupcakes on a wire rack over a baking sheet. Cover with Quick Fondant (see recipe below).

3. Pipe tube 3 stems on top of cupcake. Attach flowers with icing and add tube 65 leaves. Place on serving tray. If you wish, trim the tray with a bouquet of icing flowers.

WILTON QUICK FONDANT
  6 cups confectioners' sugar
  4½ ounces water
  2 tablespoons corn syrup
  1 teaspoon almond flavoring

Combine water and corn syrup. Add to sugar in a saucepan and stir over low heat until well-mixed and heated until just warm, about 100°F. Stir in flavoring. Place iced cakes on wire rack over baking sheet. Pour fondant, touching up bare spots with a spatula. Fondant that drips onto the baking sheet can be reheated and used again. Yields four cups fondant—enough to cover an 8″ cake or 18 heart cupcakes.

Celebrate with a sheet cake

For an anniversary, engagement party or bridal shower, this Quick & Pretty cake is easy to serve and lovely to see.

1. Make Color Flow hearts, using the recipe found on the can of Color Flow mix. Use *Celebrate! IV* heart pattern or make your own. Tape to a flat surface and cover with wax paper. Outline with tube 2 and icing straight from the batch. Thin icing and flow in. Dry at least 48 hours. Remove from wax paper and pipe names with tube 2 script.

2. Pipe drop flowers with tubes 33, 190 and 225. Add tube 2 centers.

3. Bake a 9″ x 13″ x 3″ two-layer cake. Fill, ice and place on a foil-covered board edged with Tuk-N-Ruffle. Pipe tube 16 bottom shell border. Divide long sides of cake into sixths and short sides into fourths. Drop a tube 2 guideline from point to point. Following guideline, pipe a tube 104 ribbon swag. Attach small drop flowers at points of swags with dots of icing. Add tube 65 leaves.

4. Divide top of cake into 24 sections, marking only the center of each. Secure Color Flow hearts with icing, propping with sugar cubes. They will cover the four center sections. Attach drop flowers around them and add tube 65 leaves. Figure pipe a heart at each section mark with tube 17. Add a tube 16 top shell border. Serves 24.

Put a little love in your life

Quick & Pretty

Quick & Pretty

Quick & Pretty

Share a little love!

See what simple techniques, bright tinted icing and clever use of shaped pans can do to make someone happy! These are cakes to do while the baby takes a nap, before the children come home from school, or for a spur-of-the-moment party. Everyone will love them—and you!

Bake two cute babies

One cake mix, just a little time and two fluffy bows will turn out the most talked-about shower cake you ever served.

1. Using one cake mix, bake two layers in 9″ petal pans. Ice thinly in flesh-colored buttercream. Use the *Celebrate! IV* pattern, or make your own for the faces. The boy and girl are identical except for the hair. Note that the curve of the chin corresponds to one petal curve of the pan. Outline face and features with tube 2. Pipe tube 16 strands for boy baby's hair.

2. Starting at base, cover cake sides with tube 16 stars. Pipe two rows of colored stars around outer bonnet edges on top of cake, then two rows of white stars. Continue piping stars until entire top of cake is covered. Overpipe a white edge on bonnets with tube 16. Pipe button noses with tube 12, and use same tube for blue eyes. Flatten eyes with a damp finger. Add a smile to each face with tube 2, set the cakes on a tray and place matching fluffy bows at the chins. Serves eight very generously or 16 daintily.

Bring two tulips to bloom

Why wait for spring when tulips can flower on your table tonight? It's as easy as one-two-three to create them and fun, too.

1. Bake two layers of cake in bell pans and one layer in an oval pan.

Chill the cakes. Trim off the "clapper" from the bell pans and make two notches about 2″ in from each of the wide-flaring edges. This creates petal shape of tulips. Cut two curved tulip leaves from the oval cake, one about 7½″ x 2½″ wide, the other about 5″ x 2½″. Use the curved edge of the oval as one curved edge of each leaf. Cut two long rectangles from rest of oval cake for stems. One measures 4″ x 1″, the other 4½″ x 1″.

2. Thinly ice the shapes, then mark curving lines with a toothpick to indicate petals and centers of leaves.

3. Cover all cake pieces with tube 16 stars. Let icing set, then arrange pieces on tray. Welcome Spring! Serves about 18.

Float brilliant butterflies

Why wait for summer when you can make these butterflies in just an hour or so?

1. Bake a one-layer cake in a 12″ petal pan and one in a 6″ square pan. Chill the cakes. Cut the petal cake into wedge-shaped quarters. Cut two 1″ x 6″ butterfly bodies from the 6″ cake. (Use the rest of the cake to feed eager watchers.)

2. Thinly ice the cake pieces. Transfer *Celebrate! IV* patterns to cakes. Outline patterns with tube 2, then fill in with tube 16 stars in sunny colors. Let icing set, then assemble the butterflies. Two butterflies serve about 18.

How to cover a cake smoothly

THE JOYOUS ART of cake decorating is a fascinating hobby, quite easy to master if taken step by step. Learn the basics on these two pages—then you can create many pretty cakes.

Icing is your medium

Here are the two icings needed for basic decorating. Use a regular electric mixer, not a hand mixer.

SNOW-WHITE BUTTERCREAM

Perfect for covering the cake, piping borders and simple flowers.

⅔ cup water
4 tablespoons meringue powder
1¼ cups solid white shortening, room temperature
¾ teaspoon salt
¼ teaspoon butter flavoring
½ teaspoon almond flavoring
½ teaspoon clear vanilla
11½ cups sifted confectioners' sugar

Combine water and meringue powder and whip at high speed until peaks form. Add four cups sugar, one cup at a time, beating after each addition at low speed. Alternately add shortening and remainder of sugar. Add salt and flavorings and beat at low speed until smooth. Thin with two teaspoons of white corn syrup per cup of icing for strings and leaves. To stiffen for some flowers, add a little confectioners' sugar. Yield: 8 cups. Store, well covered, in refrigerator. Bring to room temperature and rebeat to use again.

ROYAL ICING—MERINGUE

Use this for most flowers. Dries too hard for covering cakes.

3 tablespoons meringue powder
1 pound confectioners' sugar
3½ ounces warm water
½ teaspoon cream of tartar

Combine ingredients, mixing slowly, then beat at high speed for seven to ten minutes. Keep covered with a damp cloth. Rebeat to restore texture. Yield: 3½ cups.

Follow these steps for a perfectly iced cake

Secure one layer with icing to cardboard circle the same size as layer. Place on turntable or tray. If using filling, pipe a ring of icing around top edge to contain filling. Then spread filling inside ring. If filling with icing, spread to ¼" from edge of layer.

Add top layer, upside down on first. Brush crumbs from cake. Then brush with apricot glaze (heat one cup apricot jam to boiling and strain). Let dry until crust forms. This seals any other crumbs in and adds delicious flavor.

Cover·sides first. Using a long spatula, spread plenty of icing on side, building edges up slightly higher than cake. Use long, even strokes, working from bottom up.

Cover top. Mound icing in center of top and spread it out to blend with edges. Use plenty of icing, making sure cake is completely and evenly covered. Use long, even strokes.

Smooth top using a long metal ruler or piece of stiff cardboard. Pull straight across cake, bringing excess icing toward you.

Smooth sides. Hold spatula against side of cake and slowly spin turntable. If not using turntable, slowly turn tray. When icing sets, remove cake to tray or cake board.

16

Have fun with basic techniques

A few tips on baking

It's much easier to decorate if the cake has a level surface. Before putting the pans in the oven, do these three things to insure a flat level cake after baking. To prevent large air bubbles from forming while baking, lift the filled pans a few inches and drop onto the table. Then swirl the batter with a spoon from the center to the sides. Finally, pin wet terry cloth strips around the sides of the pans, then bake.

Always chill the layers after baking. This makes the cake firmer and easier to handle. If the surface is still not level, trim with a sharp knife.

Tools a decorator needs

Many of these basic tools you probably have in your own kitchen. To begin decorating you will need a pair of stainless steel mixing bowls, metal spoons for mixing and measuring, a pair of flexible spatulas, food colors and cake pans. You also need a 10″ or 12″ plastic or acrylic-coated polyester decorating bag, a coupler to go with the bag, nine or more decorating tubes and a flower nail. The coupler is especially useful as it allows you to change tubes without refilling the bag. A turntable is also a handy tool. It makes icing and decorating much faster and easier.

How to fill a decorating bag

Drop in a tube or coupler, grasp bag lightly in left hand and turn top one-third over into a cuff. Fill rest of bag with icing, using spatula. Then unfold cuff and twist tightly to seal bag.

Practice is essential

Do the exercises below on a practice board, or on the back of a pan. Simple designs, neatly done, will give a professional look to your cake.

Hold the decorating bag at just the right angle

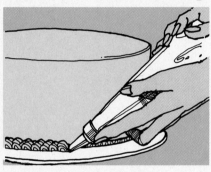

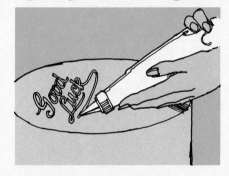

45° angle for most borders

Make short up-and-down motions with tube 14 for a tight zigzag. To make shells, touch surface lightly and squeeze heavily, letting shell build up. Pull hand down sharply, relaxing pressure and draw to a point. Join for a border by piping one over the tail of the previous one. Practice colonial scrolls using *Celebrate! IV* pattern. Follow curve with tube 4, then pipe over curve with tube 16, adding curved shell motion flourishes. Join for side of cake trim.

Almost flat for lines, script

Draw tube 3 along, making a series of short vertical lines. Make a series of "C's", slanted lines and horizontal lines. Try to make all lines the same size and thickness, with the ends cut off neatly. Now practice script using the same tube position. Try to glide over the surface without digging in and use your whole arm to make the curves. Even if your handwriting is not perfect, with practice you'll be able to pipe attractive script.

Hold bag perpendicular for dots, stars and rosettes

To pipe dots, hold bag straight up and touch tube lightly to surface. Hold in position while you squeeze and icing will begin to mound. Raise tube with it, keeping tip buried. Then stop pressure and move away. Strive for round uniform shapes. Pipe with sides touching for border. Practice swirled rosettes, moving up and away with a circular motion. Now try a fleur-de-lis. Pipe a shell, then pipe a curved shell on either side and add a star at base.

PIPE TIGHT ZIGZAG FOR BORDER

PRACTICE LINES, CURVES

PIPE DOTS. . . KEEP EVENLY SIZED

PIPE SHELLS. . . JOIN FOR BORDER

PRACTICE SCRIPT

SWIRL ROSETTES . . . JOIN FOR BORDER

PRACTICE SCROLL FOR SIDE BORDER

FLEURS-DE-LIS ARE JUST CURVED SHELLS

mark a special day

This beautiful little anniversary cake is so versatile and so easy to make. Change the message, the color or the number of candles and it can become a cake for almost any occasion. Follow the steps carefully and you'll see how quickly you can create a truly distinguished cake.

1. Bake a 10″ round, two-layer cake. Fill and ice the layers smoothly as described on previous page. When icing has set, place it on a foil-covered cardboard cake board. Then, before starting to decorate, make sure you place the cake at eye level so you can make the side and base designs accurately.

2. With a toothpick, carefully mark freehand "C" shapes on the cake top and sides so the completed pattern will cover about ⅓ of the cake. Vary the size of the "C's" to give the pattern a casual look.

3. Pipe the message on the cake top with tube 2. Be careful of the spacing, centering it on the ⅔ of the cake that won't be covered by the pattern.

You may want to mark the writing in the icing carefully with a toothpick first, then pipe over the marks.

4. Pipe cornelli lace with tube 2 within and up to the toothpick-marked pattern lines. Cornelli lace is a meandering string of icing that zigzags along for a jigsaw puzzle effect. Just make sure that the lines never touch or cross each other. This is a very easy design to pipe.

5. Pipe "C" shapes with tube 18, adding little curling flourishes to the inner curve of the ones on top with the same tube. Then pipe tube 18 star border around bottom of cake, piping on both sides of lowest "C" shapes. Also pipe tube 18 stars around top edges of cake for the top border, but only on section not covered with cornelli lace.

6. Insert slim taper into top of cake and you have created a cake you can serve to 14 with pride.

red, white and true blue

This festive cake for a Fourth of July celebration is easy to decorate, but you must measure for the side decorations very accurately. This is another very versatile cake design. Change the ornament, the message, the color and you will have a very pretty cake for just about any occasion you choose to make memorable for someone special.

1. Bake two 10″ round layers. Fill and ice smoothly as directed on the previous page. When the icing has set, transfer the cake to a cake stand or a foil-covered cardboard cake board.

2. Accuracy in dividing the side of the cake is very important, so cut a strip of paper long enough to go around the side of the cake with the ends just meeting. Divide the paper into sixteenths by folding. Fold it back and forth as you would fold a fan to keep the spacing accurate. Pin the paper onto the cake and mark the divisions with tiny dots of icing or a toothpick. Remove the paper and mark vertical lines up the cake

side at each division by pressing the edge of a spatula into the icing.

3. Before piping any design on the cake, place it at eye level. Make the side design by following the vertical lines you made in the icing. Pipe wide tube 17 zigzags, alternating red and blue zigzags around the side. Next, pipe tube 17 stars around the bottom of the cake as the base border, alternating red, white and blue stars.

4. On the top of the cake, pipe tube 3 message, being careful to space the letters evenly. If you need to, mark the lettering in the icing with a toothpick first. Then pipe tube 17 stars for the top border. To finish the cake, insert two cloth flags into the top of the cake so the staffs are crossed. This patriotic little cake serves 14.

make a birthday merrier

Here's a jolly birthday castle to make any child smile. It is simple to create when taken step-by-step.

1. To create castle towers, bake cakes in cans. Sizes you need are 5″ x 2¾″ (vegetable), 4″ x 2½″ (soup) and 3″ x 3″ (orange). Make sure cans are well-greased and floured before filling ⅔ full of batter. Cakes will mound up and mounds will be tops of towers. Also bake an 8″ x 2″ round cake. Ice can cakes and 8″ cake smoothly (follow instructions on page 17). Place 8″ cake on foil-covered cardboard cake board.

2. Pipe tube 7 bottom ball border on 8″ cake. Place tallest can cake on top of 8″ cake, positioning to rear of one side. Pipe tube 5 balls around bottom. Then place second tallest can cake to rear on other side of 8″ cake. Pipe tube 5 balls around bottom. Finally, place shortest can cake at front of 8″ cake. Pipe tube 5 balls as far around bottom as you can reach.

3. Make faces for windows on pink mints. Pipe tube 2 dots for eyes and

nose, then dip finger in cornstarch and flatten. Pipe mouth and hair with same tube. Dry.

4. With toothpick, mark window shape on can cakes. Outline shapes with tube 2 beading (a series of little dots). Attach faces in windows with dot of icing. Pipe tube 7 ball border around top of 8″ cake.

5. Cut three 5″ circles from stiff paper. Cut slit in each from edge to center of circle. Bend one into cone shape to fit top of one can cake. Trim overlap and glue together. Set on cake. Do same for other circles, fitting them to the other cakes.

6. Cut triangular banners for roofs. Glue each to cloth-covered florists' wire. Pipe message with tube 1. Pipe dot of icing on point of roof with tube 7. Let icing set a bit, then insert wire of banner into it. Hold in position until stable. To serve cake, remove castles to slice, then slice base. Serves 17.

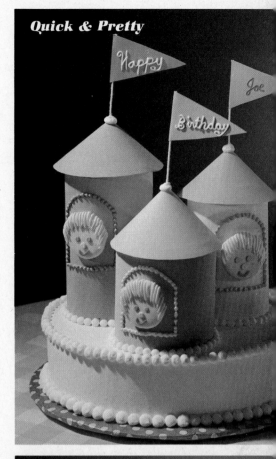

a graduation tribute

Congratulate your favorite graduate with a sheet cake topped with a star method plaque. Using this easy method, you can pipe many colorful icing "pictures".

1. Make plaque in advance. Using pattern from *Celebrate! IV Pattern Book*, tape to piece of glass or plexiglas and smoothly tape wax paper or plastic wrap over it. Pipe over all pattern lines with tube 2 and brown royal icing, then pipe tube 13 royal icing stars *very close together* to fill in design. If stars are not close together (no spaces between them) the plaque will fall apart when removed from wax paper or plastic wrap.

Pipe large tube 3 royal icing dots for eyes and nose, then flatten with finger dipped in cornstarch. Pipe tube 3 mouth. Outline mortarboard with tube 3 and pipe tassel with same tube. Dry thoroughly.

2. Bake a two-layer 9″ x 13″ cake. Fill and ice smoothly as described on page 17. Place on foil-covered cardboard rectangle. Pipe message

on side of cake with tube 2, being careful to center it.

3. Pipe tube 17 shells around top edge of cake and down the side seams. Pipe tube 17 rosettes around base of cake, then frame them by piping a tube 13 zigzag on board around base of rosettes. Pipe a tube 13 star between rosettes.

4. Cut tape and carefully turn over the dried plaque and peel off the wax paper or plastic wrap. Using the pattern as a guide, cut an oval from wax paper ¼″ smaller than plaque. Mark position of plaque on top of cake by making tiny marks in icing around wax paper oval with a toothpick. Pipe small mounds of royal icing within oval and gently place plaque in position. Pipe tube 17 shells around edge of plaque.

5. Pipe tube 17 rosettes on front, back and top of cake. Trim with tube 68 leaves. Serves 24.

These cakes are idea starters!

All the cakes here are easily adapted to the color or kind you need or like best. Start with the ideas here—then browse through this book and use your imagination!

decorate a bridal masterpiece

YES, YOU CAN DECORATE a beautiful wedding cake. It doesn't need a great deal of time or expertise, only the basics you learned on pages 16 and 17. Just remember that a tier cake is nothing but several regular size cakes put together.

1. Pipe in advance about 32 roses and 16 buds as described at right. Practice making colonial scrolls shown on page 17 before piping them on cake. Have at hand two 10″ round separator plates, four 5″ Corinthian pillars and a petite top ornament.

2. Bake two-layer tiers—6″, 10″ and 14″ round. Fill and ice as described on page 16. Place 14″ tier on a 16″ foil-covered cardboard cake board.

3. Position separator plate on 14″ tier. Press to mark icing, then lift off. Within this circle, push seven ¼″ dowel rods down to cake board, mark where rod meets cake surface, then lift to cut off exposed portion with wire cutters. Push back down until level with surface. These rods will support weight of tiers above. Attach pillars and pegs to separator plate. Push pegs into tier until plate rests on top.

Attach 10″ tier to separator plate, then insert dowel rods as for 14″ tier, but using 6″ cardboard circle to mark position. Place 6″ tier in position. Attach plate to pillars. Now begin!

4. Use tube 16 for all borders and designs. Pipe scallops around lower separator plate. Mark colonial scrolls with a toothpick on side of tier using *Celebrate! IV* pattern and leaving a 5″ open area in the front and back. Pipe as described on page 17. Pipe shells around top and bottom of tier.

5. Pipe a fleur-de-lis on front and back of 10″ tier (see page 17). Pipe stars above and at base of each. Pipe shells around top and bottom of tier. Measure tier and divide into eighths, as you did for patriotic cake on page 18. Pipe eight fleurs-de-lis around side of 6″ tier, adding star at base of each. Pipe shell border around top and bottom of tier.

6. To finish, place petite ornament on top of 6″ tier. Attach rosebud and two roses with icing. Attach roses and buds to top of 10″ tier on mound of icing forming two small sprays. Push spikes of two roses and buds into side. Pipe a mound of icing between

pillars and attach roses and buds. In center of front and back of 14″ tier, attach roses and buds with icing.

Begin at board and work up to form a triangular shape. Pipe tube 68 leaves. Serves 156.

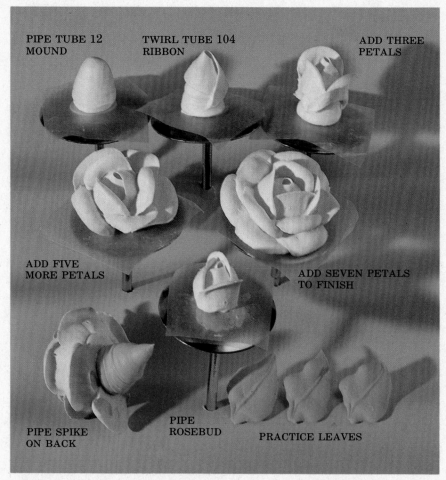

PIPE TUBE 12 MOUND   TWIRL TUBE 104 RIBBON   ADD THREE PETALS

ADD FIVE MORE PETALS   ADD SEVEN PETALS TO FINISH

PIPE SPIKE ON BACK   PIPE ROSEBUD   PRACTICE LEAVES

How to pipe a perfect rose in royal icing

The rose, most cherished flower, may look difficult to pipe—but you can do it, following the pictures and instructions. Royal icing allows you to make the flowers well in advance, and to attach some to cake sides.

1. Attach square of wax paper to number 7 nail with icing. Hold tube 12 perpendicular and pipe a dome-shaped mound.

2. Change to tube 104 and hold bag at 45° angle, wide end touching mound near top, narrow end almost straight up. Squeeze out ribbon of icing and turn nail counterclockwise. Swing tube up, around and back down.

3. Pipe row of three standing petals. Hold bag pointing from shoulder; touch wide end of tube to mound about halfway up with narrow end

turned out slightly. For each petal, turn nail counterclockwise and move tube up and down in half-moon arch.

4. Pipe a row of five petals the same as first row, but turning narrow end out even more.

5. Pipe seven overlapping petals, pointing narrow end out farther. Slide wax paper off nail to dry.

6. When dry, peel off paper and pipe tube 6 spike on back of four roses.

7. To make a bud, follow steps 1 through 3 above, but make beginning mound smaller.

8. To make leaves, use softened icing and tube 68. Touch to surface and squeeze to build up a base. Then gradually pull away, relaxing pressure halfway. Discontinue pressure, lift tube and draw leaf to a point.

Rosy Future
A bridal masterpiece

Decorate
a lavish New Year's cake
Serve it with love

Create this beautiful cake trimmed with pineapples, the symbol of hospitality, and other fruit to wish good luck and good fortune in the new year to those you love. It is topped with an adorable New Year's baby molded of gum paste in the Wilton People Molds. These three-part molds have added even more excitement to the fascinating art of gum paste.

Here we show you just how to make little New Year. Soon you'll be molding many more figurines for your own showpieces.

Gum paste needs

To create gum paste figures, you will need a small artist's brush, florists' wire, wire cutters, an X-acto or other sharp knife, powdered pastels (pastel sticks shaved with a sharp knife), clear acrylic spray glaze and Wilton People Molds. You will also need a recipe of gum paste.

GUM PASTE RECIPE
1 tablespoon Gum-tex™ or
    tragacanth gum
1 heaping tablespoon glucose
3 tablespoons warm water
1 pound confectioners' sugar
    (or more)

1. Mix tragacanth gum and glucose until smooth and dissolved. Add warm water one tablespoon at a time. Stir in small amounts of confectioners' sugar until you can work mixture with your hands. Continue adding small amounts of sugar until you have added about ¾ pound.

2. Since gum paste handles best when aged, store in plastic bag at least overnight, then break off a piece and work in more sugar until the mixture is pliable but not sticky.

3. To store for a length of time, place gum paste in a plastic bag in a covered container to prevent drying. It will keep several months.

4. To color, apply a small amount of paste color to a piece of gum paste

with a toothpick. Then knead the piece until the tint is evenly spread.

5. To roll gum paste, dust the work surface with cornstarch. Take a small piece of gum paste, keeping the rest well-covered, and work it in your hands. Place it on the cornstarch-dusted area, dust rolling pin with cornstarch and roll out the gum paste to the desired thickness. Remember to roll only one small piece at a time to prevent drying.

6. To attach two wet gum paste pieces, or one wet and one dry, brush with a small amount of egg white and press gently together.

Mold the figure

Making darling, perfectly-proportioned little people is much easier than before when you use Wilton People Molds. These three-part molds make legs and lower body, head and torso, and arms.

Use the five-year old child molds to create the New Year's baby. Carefully read the instruction booklet that accompanies the molds before starting to mold the figure. Follow standing figure directions.

Mold the legs and lower body first. Position legs so the figure stands firmly. Mold head and torso after legs have dried. Position on top of legs. Using a sharp knife and pointed stick, carefully open the mouth. Dry. Mold arms one at a time. Position carefully and prop with cotton balls.

Make up the face

Blush the cheeks with deep flesh-colored powdered pastel and a soft, dry brush.

Do the eyes next. With watered-down copper color, brush in shadow above the eye. Whiten the eye socket with a white pencil. Designate the pupil with a dot of copper color. Paint in iris of eye. Darken the pupil, then paint in a thin line at the top of the eye socket for eyelashes. Make the highlight in the eye with the point of a sharp knife.

Paint the lips with thinned food color, starting with the lower one. Paint in hairline with royal icing.

Finish the figure

1. Roll out gum paste as thin as possible and cut tunic using *Celebrate! IV* pattern. Lay tunic on a piece of foam toweling and roll bottom portion with modeling stick 2 so it will flare out. Brush upper portion of tunic with egg white and wrap around figure with the seam in back. Trim seam so edges butt. Position the lower part of the tunic in soft folds. Trim a rounded neckline and armholes with a sharp knife. Dry.

2. Roll a thin cylinder of gum paste about 1″ long for horn. Hollow one end with a pointed stick and dry.

3. Attach arms in position with a small piece of gum paste dipped in egg white. Prop arms with cotton until dry. Place horn in hands and

secure with tiny dots of royal icing.

4. Pipe dot trim on tunic hem with tube 1s and around neckline and armholes. Add wispy tube 1 hair. Dry, then spray figure with two coats of clear acrylic spray glaze to seal out moisture.

5. Every gum paste figure to be used on a cake must be set on a plastic, cardboard or styrofoam base. Otherwise, the moisture in the buttercream icing will cause the gum paste to "melt." Plaque is added during cake assembly.

WANT TO KNOW MORE about making gum paste people? *The Wilton Way of Cake Decorating, Volume Two* has a complete, full-color chapter showing how to create whimsical and inspiring action figures in gum paste.

Model marzipan fruits

Hand-model marzipan fruits using the recipe below. Make about two pineapples, six bananas, six apples, six oranges and twelve plums. Pineapples are 1¼″ x 1¼″, other fruits proportionately smaller.

1. Score pineapples with a spatula and press in with a star tube to create texture. Push a toothpick into

the top of the pineapple. Tops are triangular pieces of marzipan wrapped around the toothpick and secured with egg white. Bend outward for a natural look. Brush pineapple with food color thinned with kirschwasser or other liqueur.

2. Model bananas and paint on details with food coloring thinned with kirschwasser. Make apples and push a clove in the bottom and press in a hole in the top. Make oranges like apples, but roll on grater for texture. Model oval plums and press in a line with a spatula.

3. When all fruits are modeled, brush them with syrup glaze (mix ½ cup corn syrup, 1 cup water and bring to a boil) for a soft shine.

MARZIPAN RECIPE

   1 cup almond paste (8 ounce can)
   2 egg whites, unbeaten
   3 cups confectioners' sugar
   ½ teaspoon vanilla or
      rum flavoring

Knead almond paste by hand in bowl. Add egg whites and mix well. Knead in confectioners' sugar, one cup at a time, and flavoring until marzipan feels like heavy pie dough. Knead food colors into marzipan one

drop at a time until a natural shade is achieved.

To store, cover with plastic wrap and place in a tightly sealed container in the refrigerator. It will keep for months. After storing, bring to room temperature. If still too stiff to work, soften with a drop or two of warmed corn syrup.

Make stylized lattice pineapples

Turn the egg cupcake pan over and grease the backs of the eggs with solid white vegetable shortening. With tube 2 and royal icing, pipe a line about ½″ up from the base of the egg, then pipe lattice. Dry. You will need 16 lattice pineapples. To remove from pan, place in a warm oven about ½ minute to melt shortening and then carefully remove lattice.

Make gum paste scroll

Roll out a piece of gum paste very thin and cut scroll using *Celebrate! IV* pattern. Roll edges and dry. Pipe New Year's message with tube 1.

Assemble the cake

Now that the component parts are made, the cake is easy to assemble.

1. Bake an oval tier, 3″ high and a 9″ x 13″ tier, 4″ high. Ice with buttercream and assemble on a foil-covered board. Ice a cardboard oval, about 3″ x 4″ with royal icing as a base for the New Year's baby to stand on. Place it on top of the oval tier, near the front edge. Conceal it with more icing.

2. Pipe a tube 18 reverse shell border around base of cake. With tube 2, pipe a line of icing around the lattice pineapples and attach around side of base tier. Position five on each long side and three on each short side. Pipe pineapple tops with tube 326. Add a tube 16 top shell border.

3. On oval tier, pipe a tube 16 reverse shell border around base and a tube 16 top shell border. Secure gum paste scroll to side of tier with icing. Insert candles into top and surround with a froth of tube 18 shells.

4. Secure marzipan fruits to top of base tier with dots of icing. Attach New Year's baby to cardboard on top of oval tier with dots of royal icing on his feet. Light the candles and your glorious cake is ready to greet the new year! Serves 36.

AND FOR THANKSGIVING, this cake without the gum paste figure, would be an excellent choice to serve after the turkey dinner.

Greet the New Year with a wish for sunny days

The sundial on this sunny cake is patterned after one crafted in the eighteenth century. Since clocks were very expensive at this time, small sundials were set on window sills to tell the time on a sunny day.

Make Color Flow cake top

Tape *Celebrate! IV* patterns to a flat surface and cover smoothly with wax paper. Outline with tube 2 and icing straight from the batch. Then thin icing as directed on page 145. Flow in and place pieces under a heat lamp placed two feet above them for two hours. This gives a shiny finish. Complete drying for at least 48 hours.

Using pattern as a guide, pipe details with tube 2 and royal icing. Let dry thoroughly. On triangular piece, outline again when dry with tube 2. Dry, turn over and outline the other side. When dry, attach to sundial as shown, using royal icing.

Decorate the cake

After the sundial is made, the cake is simple to decorate.

1. Bake a 10″ × 4″ round, two-layer cake. Ice smoothly and place on a serving tray or foil-covered board.

2. Cut a 2″ wide strip of paper long enough to go around cake with ends just meeting. Divide into twelve equal sections by folding like a fan, then cut a double scallop pattern. Pin pattern around side of cake and mark scallops with a toothpick.

3. Pipe tube 16 stars very close together to cover the section of the cake below the scallops. Then pipe tube 16 stars above the scallops on the side of the cake and extending 2½″ in on the top of the cake.

4. Place sundial in center of cake, attaching with mounds of royal icing piped in the smoothly iced section of the cake top. A cheerful cake to brighten a winter day that serves 14.

Put a little love in your life

Celebrate!®

MARCH/APRIL...springtime begins!

HAPPY EASTER!

Decorating directions on page 34

Plan a spring wedding reception

YES, YOU CAN PREPARE this elegant reception buffet that features food almost everyone will love, attractively presented. The menu is suitable for a wedding breakfast, luncheon or supper and is just as appropriate for an anniversary party or other important celebration.

Planning is the key to any successful party. Everything on this menu, even the salad, may be made ahead of time. Only ordinary household equipment that you have in your own kitchen is needed.

Reception menu
Creamed Turkey
in Crisp Noodle Baskets
Peas and Pearl Onions in
Butter Sauce
Carrots with Grand Marnier Glaze
Wedding Salad
Pickled Peach Slices, Black Olives
Tiny Sweet Pickles
Hot Buttered Rolls
Wedding Cake   Ice Cream Balls
Champagne or Fruit Punch
Coffee

Economy was kept in mind while planning this menu, but everything is delicious and given a fresh unusual garnish or flavor.

Use your nicest china and silver and grace the table with a beautiful flower arrangement. If you don't have enough china or serving pieces, these may be rented. Guests can help themselves although it is wise to have someone standing by to act as hostess. Set up smaller tables for the guests to eat at, and serve coffee and dessert at the tables. A fork, dessert fork and spoon for each guest is all the flat silver needed.

It is prettier and more practical for the wedding cake to be set on its own separate table. Please turn the page for recipes and instructions.

How to prepare and serve an elegant reception buffet

The most important thing to remember if you are going to prepare and serve a reception buffet is to plan all the details well in advance. A well-planned reception will always run smoothly and be enjoyable for you *and* the guests.

First count the guest list so you can plan the amount of food needed. Each recipe serves 50. If you will be serving 100 guests, do not double the recipes, make them twice instead. In planning the number of dinner rolls to be served, figure one and a half per person. Butter them the day before, refrigerate, and heat in oven before serving.

Be sure you have pots and serving pieces large enough to hold the food during and after the preparation. All of the recipes can be made in advance and refrigerated, then reheated before serving. Follow the instructions in each recipe for doing this. Form the ice cream into balls ahead of time and freeze solidly. Eight quarts are needed for 50 servings, ½ cup each.

For 50 guests, one long buffet table should be set up (use two for 100 guests). A minimum of four people should be helping—one in the kitchen heating the food, one at the table to serve, and two or more to remove the plates and serve dessert. For 100 guests, seven people are needed—one in the kitchen, one at each of the two tables and four or more to remove plates.

Plan your reception well, center the buffet table with a lovely bouquet and enjoy the party!

Creamed Turkey

This is an elegant main dish for a wedding reception buffet. It's easy to serve and can be made ahead, refrigerated and reheated.

    2 turkey breasts (about 5 pounds each)
    2 quarts water
    2⅔ cups sliced mushrooms
    2¼ pounds butter
    5⅓ cups milk
    5⅓ cups half-and-half
    4 cups all-purpose flour
    2 tablespoons salt
    1½ teaspoons white pepper
    2 cups chopped pimento, drained on paper towels
    2 cups chopped green pepper
    12 hard-cooked eggs, diced
    50 Crisp Noodle Baskets (see recipe below)

1. Place turkey breasts in a very large pot and add water. (Be sure pot is large enough as amount of liquid will double as it cooks out of the turkey.) Cover pot, bring to boiling, and simmer about 2 hours or until internal temperature reaches 190°F. Cool, remove meat from bones and cut into ¾″ pieces. Reserve 14½ cups of cooking liquid.

2. Sauté mushrooms in ¼ pound of the butter; set aside.

3. Combine reserved cooking liquid from turkey, milk, and half-and-half.

Heat thoroughly.

4. Meanwhile, melt remaining 2 pounds of butter. Blend in flour, salt and pepper. Heat until bubbly. Slowly add hot liquid, stirring until smooth. Cook slowly until thickened and smooth, stirring constantly. Stir in turkey pieces and sautéed mushrooms. Heat thoroughly. At this point the mixture can be cooled, refrigerated and reheated later. When reheating, thin sauce with milk to original consistency.

5. When ready to serve, gently mix in chopped pimento, green pepper and diced eggs. Allow about ½ cup of mixture for each Crisp Noodle Basket. Makes about 50 servings.

Crisp Noodle Baskets

These crunchy little baskets offer a nice contrast to the creamed turkey. They're easy to make, but having a helper makes the work go faster.

    3 pounds vermicelli (extra-thin spaghetti)
    Cooking Oil
    Salt

1. Cook the vermicelli one pound at a time. Break the strands into 2″ lengths and add to rapidly boiling salted water. Boil about five minutes, or until vermicelli drapes easily over a spoon handle. Drain in a colander, rinse with cold water and drain again.

2. Heat the oil gradually to 390°F. Use a straight-sided pan high enough to allow 3″ above the surface of the oil, and 4″ below it to bottom of pan. This will determine amount of oil. (When finished, oil can be strained for future use.) If you are not using a thermometer, test temperature by dropping a 1″ square of bread into oil. It should brown in 40 seconds.

3. Fluff the cooked vermicelli with your hands. Use two tea strainers, one 3″ in diameter and the other 2½″ in diameter to form the baskets— or you may use a set of metal baskets made for this purpose. Before making the first basket, dip the strainers into the oil. Lightly heap vermicelli into the larger one, pressing against sides, then set smaller strainer into larger. Immerse strainers into hot oil. Foaming will soon subside. Cook until golden, about three and a half minutes. Keep oil at 390°F.

4. Drain baskets on paper towels and sprinkle each with salt. To remove from strainers, take off larger strainer and tap rim of the smaller

one. Basket will drop·out. Store as long as several days in a loosely covered container at room temperature. Reheat in a 250°F oven for 15 or 20 minutes. Serve wrapped in a napkin on a tray. This recipe makes 60 or more 3″ baskets. If serving more than 50 guests, each pound of vermicelli will make 20 or more baskets.

Wedding Salad

Be sure to make this delightful, creamy salad at least the day before to blend the flavors.

    ½ cup sugar
    2 tablespoons flour
    ¼ cup vinegar
    4 egg whites
    4 cups whipping cream
    2 quarts shredded cabbage
        (about 2 pounds)
    8 ounces large marshmallows,
        cut in pieces
    2 cans (20 ounces each) crushed
        pineapple, drained
    2 cups slivered blanched
        almonds
    Pineapple chunks and parsley
        for garnish

1. Combine sugar and flour in a small saucepan; stir in vinegar. Cook until thick. Place in a large bowl and set aside to cool.

2. Beat egg whites until stiff, not dry, peaks form. Whip cream, 1 cup at a time, until soft peaks form. Fold beaten egg whites and whipped cream into cooled cooked mixture.

3. Combine cabbage, marshmallows, pineapple, and almonds; add dressing and mix well. Chill thoroughly, at least overnight. Allow ½ cup for each serving. About 50 servings.

Glazed Carrots

    8½ pounds fresh carrots, pared
        and cut, or frozen baby
        carrots
    ½ cup butter
    1 cup orange juice
    3 tablespoons honey
    2 teaspoons ground ginger
    2 teaspoons salt
    1 cup grand-marnier

1. Cook carrots in a small amount of boiling salted water until tender; drain.

2. Melt butter and blend in orange juice, honey and a mixture of ginger and salt.

3. Add drained carrots and warm over low heat, turning carrots occasionally to coat with sauce. Can be made ahead and refrigerated at this point, then reheated.

4. Just before serving, pour grand-marnier over carrots and heat. Allow about ⅓ cup for each serving. About 50 servings.

Buttered Peas and Onions

    7½ pounds frozen baby peas
    2 jars (16 ounces each) small
        sweet whole onions, drained
    Butter Sauce (recipe below)

1. Cook peas as directed on package; drain. Stir in Butter Sauce.

2. Gently mix onions with cooked peas and warm over low heat. Allow about ⅓ cup for each serving. Makes about 50 servings. Note: To reheat peas, place over very low heat and stir gently; add a small amount of water if needed.

Butter Sauce

    ¾ cup butter
    6 tablespoons flour
    1½ teaspoons salt
    ¼ teaspoon paprika
    Dash cayenne pepper
    3 cups water

1. Melt butter in medium saucepan. Stir in flour, salt, paprika ·and cayenne pepper.

2. Add water and cook until mixture boils and thickens, stirring constantly. Makes 3 cups sauce.

Wedding Pound Cake

This recipe makes a delicious, firm cake that holds together well when building a tier cake.

    4 cups sifted all-purpose flour
    2 teaspoons baking powder
    1 teaspoon salt
    ½ teaspoon ground mace
    2 cups butter
    1 tablespoon vanilla extract
    2¼ cups sugar
    8 large eggs
    ½ cup milk

1. Plan your cake design, determining tier sizes. Page 156 tells how to do this. See chart below for pan sizes, amount of batter and baking time. Grease and flour desired pans.

2. Sift together flour, baking powder, salt and mace; set aside.

3. Cream butter with vanilla extract until softened. Gradually add sugar, beating until fluffy. Add eggs, one at a time, beating thoroughly after each addition, then until mixture is light and fluffy.

4. Add dry ingredients alternately in thirds with the milk in halves to creamed mixture, mixing only until smooth after each addition.

5. Fill the pans with batter as indi-

cated. Repeat recipe as needed for amount of batter to fill pans.

6. Bake at 300°F for the time indicated, or until a wooden pick inserted in center comes out clean.

7. Cool cake layers in pans on wire racks ten minutes for 6″ and 8″ pans and 20 minutes for 12″ pans. Turn out of pans and cool thoroughly on wire racks. About 9¼ cups batter.

PANS (2″ DEEP)	AMOUNT OF BATTER	BAKING TIME
6″ round	1¾ to 2 cups	40 to 50 minutes
8″ round	3½ to 4 cups	55 to 60 minutes
12″ round	8 cups	1 hour

Best-ever Applesauce Fruitcake*

A marvelous recipe for the groom's cake shown on page 76.

    3 cups all-purpose flour
    2 teaspoons baking soda
    1 teaspoon baking powder
    ½ teaspoon ground cloves
    ½ teaspoon nutmeg
    ½ teaspoon cinnamon
    ½ teaspoon salt
    1 pound candied cherries
    ½ pound mixed candied fruit
    ½ pound candied pineapple
    ¾ cup dates
    1 cup raisins
    1½ cups pecans
    1½ cups walnuts
    ½ cup butter
    1 cup sugar
    2 eggs
    ½ cup grape juice
    1½ cups applesauce

1. Sift and mix flour, baking soda, baking powder, spices and salt.

2. Cut up fruit and coarsely chop nuts. Mix fruit and nuts.

3. Cream butter and sugar. Add eggs and beat well.

4. Beating until blended after each addition, alternately add dry ingredients and grape juice to creamed mixture. Mix in fruit, nuts and applesauce.

5. Turn into a greased 11″ ring pan. Bake at 275°F about 2¼ hours.

6. Run a knife around tube and sides and let set about 10 minutes in pan. Remove cake and cool thoroughly. Keeps well for about 2 months or more when tightly wrapped; it also freezes well. Recipe yields one six pound fruitcake.

*A thank you to Helen Wooldridge of Las Cruces, New Mexico, for this delicious recipe.

Signs of the season

. . . a little lamb

Here's a new technique for all you artistic decorators that helps you create show-off cakes just as fresh as spring! These little figures are "sculptured" from icing over a florists' wire armature. Turn to page 42 for the picture story on how to make them.

We show Mary and her companion actual size so you can see every detail of her embroidered apron and pantaloons and the wooly texture of the little lamb. The cake is a stage for the nursery rhyme figures.

1. Make the trims in advance. Roll out gum paste (recipe, page 22) and cut the banner, using *Celebrate! IV* pattern, or make your own. Dry flat about 24 hours. Pipe the script with tube 2. When dry, turn over and pipe a royal icing spike in the center and on both ends of the banner. If you prefer, you may make the banner in the Color Flow technique. Pipe tube 190 royal icing drop flowers and add tube 2 centers. Dry.

2. Bake and fill a two-layer 8″ square cake. Ice the sides smoothly in a dainty blue. Ice the top green and pat with a clean damp sponge. Edge the base with tube 18 shells and the top with tube 16. Push in banner on mounds of icing and attach flowers. Pipe tube 65 leaves. Set Mary and the little lamb on top. A prize-winning cake that serves twelve.

Mary had a little lamb

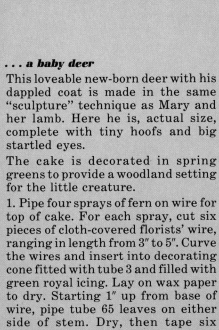

. . . a baby deer

This loveable new-born deer with his dappled coat is made in the same "sculpture" technique as Mary and her lamb. Here he is, actual size, complete with tiny hoofs and big startled eyes.

The cake is decorated in spring greens to provide a woodland setting for the little creature.

1. Pipe four sprays of fern on wire for top of cake. For each spray, cut six pieces of cloth-covered florists' wire, ranging in length from 3″ to 5″. Curve the wires and insert into decorating cone fitted with tube 3 and filled with green royal icing. Lay on wax paper to dry. Starting 1″ up from base of wire, pipe tube 65 leaves on either side of stem. Dry, then tape six fronds together with floral tape.

2. Bake and fill a two-layer oval cake. Ice thickly in buttercream, then pat all over with a clean damp sponge. Divide cake into eighths and mark at base. Pipe a spray of six curved tube 3 stems on side of cake at each marked point. Pipe tube 65 leaves on stems, starting at base. Finish with a tube 18 shell border.

Set the baby deer on top and display your spring creation to an admiring audience. Serves twelve.

Turn to page 42 for directions for making the deer.

Signs of the season

An Easter centerpiece

Build a cute centerpiece from cookies! The children will love this hard-working 3-D bunny who tugs birds and a butterfly in an Easter egg cart.

1. Bake the cookies using roll-out recipe (page 147) or your own favorite. Use *Celebrate! IV* pattern for the bunny. Cut two shapes with the Giant Egg cookie cutter, two 2½″ circles, two 1½″ daisies, six 1″ hearts, two bird and one butterfly cookies. Cut a shallow curve from top of each egg-shaped cookie before baking. Using the oval pan as pattern, cut a 9″ x 7″ oval for the cookie base.

2. Make royal icing drop flowers using tube 225. Add tube 2 centers and dry.

3. Outline all cookies except base oval with Color Flow icing and tube 2. Fill in with thinned icing. When thoroughly dry, ice reverse side of all cookies except daisies the same way. Add details to bunny and birds with tube 2. Pipe fluffy tail on bunny with tube 13. Ice base oval cookie and pat with clean damp sponge.

4. Use royal icing as "glue" to assemble the centerpiece. Attach base oval to foil-covered board. Trim

wheels with daisy cookies and drop flowers. Join egg shapes and secure ribbon. Attach one wheel to each egg shape. Add heart cookies. Assemble parts of bunny. Let all dry.

Set cart upright on base oval, brace with sugar cubes between wheels and attach with icing. Set bunny in front of cart, secure ribbon bow between paws and anchor with icing. Add butterflies and birds. Garnish with drop flowers. Trim flowers with tube 65 leaves. Place in the center of table for Easter morning breakfast.

Chirping chicks

Surprise everyone Easter morning with a clutch of baby chickens on cupcake nests! They're easy and fun to model in marzipan.

1. Make a batch of marzipan (recipe page 23), tint yellow, and roll about half of it into a long cylinder ¾″ in diameter. Cut off a ¾″ length and roll it between your palms into a ball for the head. Cut off about 1½″ and roll it into a pear shape. Flatten the small end of the pear and lift it for the tail. Cut a "V" on each side of body for wings, then cut shallow notches on wings and tail with a paring knife. Attach head to body by brushing with egg white, then securing with a turning motion. Let dry at least 24 hours. This method of starting with a cylinder assures a uniform size.

Brush on a soft shine with syrup glaze. (Bring ½ cup of white corn syrup mixed with one cup of water to a boil.) Pipe the beaks and blue eyes with royal icing and tube 2.

2. Bake cupcakes, using a mix or your favorite recipe. Swirl tops with icing, then dip in tinted coconut. Set chicks on cupcakes.

Easter rabbits

Bake a whole family of fluffy white bunnies and dress them up with spring flowers!

1. Bake rabbits in Small Wonder Molds. Make pointed oval pattern for ears, about ¾″ wide and 2½″ long. Cut two pieces for each ear from light cardboard. Glue a toothpick, point extending about 1½″, between ear pieces. Brush front of ears with thinned pink icing, then edge with tube 16 stars. When dry, turn over and cover back of ears with stars. Make drop flowers with tubes 131 and 129. Add tube 2 centers.

2. Set each Wonder Mold on its own cake circle. Outline rabbits' eyes, nose and mouth freehand with tube 3. Push toothpicks on ears into cakes. Cover cakes with tube 16 stars, overpiping rounded cheeks. Pipe eyes and nose with tube 10, then flatten with a damp fingertip. Over-pipe mouth with tube 3 and pipe a tube 46 tooth. Secure drop flowers with icing and trim with tube 65 leaves.

For an instant centerpiece, just set the chick cupcakes and rabbits on a two-tiered tray.

Trim Easter eggs with lavish sculptured designs

Here's a fresh new way to decorate eggs using gum paste Baroque Mold designs as trims.

Molding the eggs

Mold the eggs of sugar, summer coating or tempered chocolate.

To mold with summer coating or tempered chocolate (page 44), melt in the top of a double boiler and fill the halves of an egg mold. Let set until a shell forms, then tip mold to drain the excess. Let harden and remove from mold. To attach the halves, press the edges on a warmed cookie sheet, then press together.

Making Baroque trims

Using gum paste (recipe, page 22) and Baroque Gum Paste Molds, mold the designs for the eggs as described in the instruction booklet that accompanies the molds. Attach wet designs to egg with egg white.

Trimming the eggs

Using the pictures as a guide, trim the eggs as described below.

1. Mold a 4½" sugar egg and a bell for the base. Trim off top of bell. Attach with royal icing and pipe tube 2 beading at seam. Trim with Regalia side plumes and center flowers. Add tube 102 wild flowers and tube 66 leaves.

2. Mold a 3" sugar egg and a smaller egg half for the base. While egg is wet, score a circle the same size as Laurel Wreath design on one half. Remove this circle when scooping out center. Attach a small bouquet of violets and leaves inside one half of egg with royal icing. Then attach egg halves and secure to base. Pipe tube 2 beading on base. Add Laurel Wreaths, violets and leaves.

3. Mold a 5" summer coating egg. Make base with four Regalia center shells, attaching with egg white. Dry. Secure egg to base with royal icing. Trim with Scroll, drop flowers and leaves. Add tube 1s message.

4. Mold a 5" sugar egg. For base, cut bottom curls off Mantle designs and dry flat. Attach rest of design on either side of bottom of egg. Support egg on piece of styrofoam and attach bottom curls with royal icing as legs. Add complete and partial Mantle designs, drop flowers and leaves.

5. Mold a 3" chocolate egg. For base, cut center and a wedge from Rose Window to form collar and dry. Attach egg and add tube 3 beading. For top, cut every other curve from edge of Rose Window and attach. Trim with tube 3 and add tube 1 strings.

6. Mold a 3" summer coating egg. Base is a half of a small sugar egg painted with royal icing and trimmed with tube 2. Trim egg with complete and partial Laurel Wreaths. Add flowers and leaves.

7. Mold a 4½" sugar egg. Use a smaller half-egg for base and trim with tube 1. Attach Classic Shell and trim seam with portions of Laurel Wreaths. Add strings, rose and leaves.

8. Mold a 4½" chocolate egg. Make base the same as Egg #4. Add two Acanthus designs at top, daisies and leaves.

Signs of the season: Quick & Pretty cakes

Decorate these two darling cakes quickly and easily to celebrate St. Patrick's Day and Easter. The family will love them.

A winsome Irish colleen

1. Skirt is a small Wonder Mold, two marshmallows form head and bodice. Ice with a thin coat of icing, then assemble with toothpicks. Mark apron with a toothpick, then pipe apron, dress and hat with tube 14 stars. Pipe face, hair and buttons with tube 2. Figure pipe arms and feet with tube 2A, hands with tube 7. Add a tube 101 ruffle at shoulder, on apron and hat. Pipe a tube 101s shamrock on apron.

2. Bake, fill and ice a 10″ × 4″ round two-layer cake. Pipe tube 124 ruffled ribbon border around base. Divide side of cake into sixths and pipe four tube 2 stems at each division. Pipe tube 102 shamrocks on stems and add a tube 103 bow. Pipe tube 2 message. Add a tube 103 ruffled ribbon top border. Position colleen. Serves 14 guests.

A cheerful bunny

1. Bake single-layer 9″ heart and oval cakes. Round off point of heart. Cut two ears about 9″ × 3″ using edge of oval as one side of ear. Trim to fit against head. Use rest of oval to cut bow tie. Assemble on a 22″ × 13″ foil-covered oval board.

2. Ice cake with a thin coat of buttercream icing. Mark inside of ears, face and stripes on tie with a toothpick. Pipe tube 16 stars on inside of ears and bow tie. Cover outside of ears and face with tube 18 stars. Build up muzzle.

3. Pipe eyes and nose with tube 1A and flatten with a damp finger. Pipe mouth with tube 5. Glaze eyes by brushing with corn syrup. Ice pieces of uncooked thin spaghetti and insert for whiskers. Serves about 24.

Pose these delicate Easter lilies on a springtime cake

Wouldn't you think the flowers on this lovely cake are real lilies? They're fashioned of gum paste, using a lily cutter and a quick new method that's a joy to learn.

If you've held back from making gum paste flowers because you thought the technique was too difficult or time-taking, this stream-lined method will surprise and delight you. Even simple cakes trimmed with gum paste flowers are real showpieces—and you'll gain a reputation as an artist-decorator. Sprays of gum paste flowers offer a bonus, too. Before cutting the cake, lift them off to present to the honored guest. They'll be a treasured, lasting memento of the party.

How to create the lilies

You will need about a dozen Easter lilies and three buds.

1. Roll out a piece of gum paste (recipe, page 22) 1/16" thick. Cut flower with lily cutter. Attach the two long sides with egg white, smooth seam and shape into cone with modeling stick 2.

2. Bend petals outward and place on piece of foam toweling. Curl petals with modeling stick 3. Insert cotton ball into cone, then make hole in point of cone. Dry upside down, then remove cotton.

3. For center, tape together one 5" piece of thick florists' wire and six 1½" pieces of thin florists' wire as pictured. Insert thick wire into a decorating bag fitted with tube 4 and cover with icing. Pipe three tube 4 dots on top. Cover thin wires with icing using tube 2. Dry. Insert stem through hole in flower. Wrap stem with floral tape.

4. Make bud with a thick piece of florists' wire bent at a 90° angle and a gum paste cylinder, 1¼" x ⅜". Hand-model cylinder to form bud shape, dip wire in egg white and insert into bud. Dry. Wrap stem and base of bud with floral tape.

5. Roll out gum paste 1/16" thick and cut with lily leaf cutter. Cut this piece into thirds and attach a piece of florists' wire to back with egg white. Pinch end of leaf around wire and bend leaf. Dry. Tape lilies, leaves and

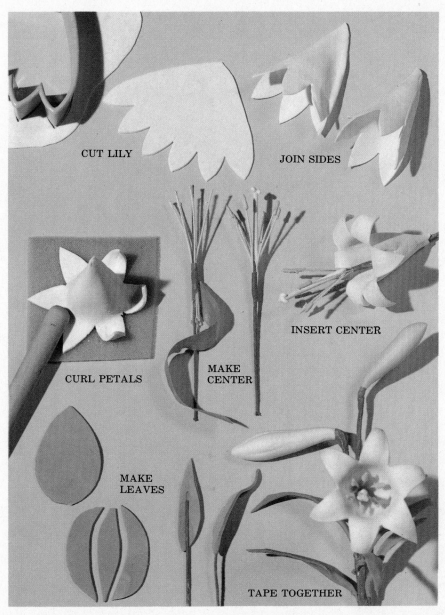

CUT LILY

JOIN SIDES

CURL PETALS

MAKE CENTER

INSERT CENTER

MAKE LEAVES

TAPE TOGETHER

buds together with floral tape into two sprays.

How to decorate the cake

1. Using Celebrate! IV pattern, cut oval from gum paste and dry on egg pan, dusted with cornstarch.

2. Bake a pound cake in the two halves of egg pan. Fill and ice egg smoothly. Let icing set, then secure to tray with icing.

3. Pipe a tube 104 ribbon swag around seam of egg. Pipe tube 2 beading in a scallop shape above swag. Attach gum paste oval to top of cake with dots of icing and pipe tube 1 lettering and tube 2 beading around edge.

4. To attach lilies, insert a dowel rod on an angle into the cake next to the gum paste oval. Leave about 1" sticking out of cake. Set spray of lilies on cake so dowel rod is between stems and supports main weight of spray. Insert toothpicks into cake to support rest of spray. Lay second spray on the tray. Serves twelve.

LIKE TO LEARN MORE about making gum paste flowers? *The Wilton Way of Cake Decorating, Volume Two* contains two full-color chapters of instructions and beautiful ways to arrange the flowers as lasting decorations. There are five color portraits of flower-trimmed cakes, too.

37

Trim these two springtime cakes with blossoms to announce an engagement, grace a shower table or star as the wedding cake itself!

Wreath of roses

1. Pipe about two dozen royal icing roses and six buds with tube 104. Pipe the centers in palest yellow and the outer petals in white. Pipe tube 67 leaves on wire, dry, then bind with floral tape into groups of three. Mount six roses on wire stems.

2. Bake a single-layer 12" round tier and a two-layer oval tier. Fill and ice with buttercream. Assemble the tiers, using dowel rods in round tier to support tier above.

Edge round tier with tube 8 balls at base, tube 6 balls at top. Pipe base border on oval tier with tube 6, top border with tube 5. Do the script and little heart with tube 2.

3. Make a cluster of three wired roses and leaves by taping stems together with floral tape. Insert a Flower Spike on side of cake just at base of oval tier, and insert cluster. Add a cluster on other side of cake. Attach roses and buds with icing on tops of tiers to form a wreath. Trim with tube 67 leaves. Tie ribbon bows on three tapers and push into cake. Serves 24 at a party, 64 at a wedding.

Flowery cakes for love's celebrations

Something blue

1. Make double daisies. Using tube 101, pipe 90 eight-petaled daisies making each petal with three strokes of the tube. Dry within curved surface. Now pipe 90 more daisies and dry flat. Attach curved flowers to flat ones with a dot of icing to form double daisy. Pipe a dot of icing in center of flower and insert artificial stamens. Mount ten daisies on wire stems.

2. Make lace and lattice pieces using patterns, tube 2 and royal icing. Make four right and four left half-hearts, four ovals and two hearts dried on 8″ curve, and one flat heart.

Pipe 200 lace pieces. Form florists' wire into a "V" shape and attach flat heart to it with icing.

3. Bake oval and 12″ square two-layer tiers. Fill and ice with buttercream and assemble on ruffle-edged board. On base tier, pipe tube 9 bottom bulb border and tube 7 top bulb border. Pipe tube 6 bulb borders on base and top of oval tier.

4. Insert Flower Spike into center of oval tier. Push wire on flat heart into cake behind it. Set White Bird in front of heart and arrange wired daisies in Flower Spike. Add more flowers, securing with icing. Attach curved hearts to front and back of oval tier with dots of icing. Bead edges with tube 2, attaching a lace piece at an angle after piping a few beads. Attach oval curved lattice to square tier, adding lace pieces the same way.

Run a line of icing down corner of square tier and set in half-heart at right angles. Pipe tube 2 beading on inner edge. Do the same with second half-heart and add beading where the two join. Complete other three corners the same way. Trim with daisies, attaching with icing. Serves 100 at a wedding, 48 at a party.

Beautiful as a blossom . . .

this sweet flower-shaped bassinet that you make from gum paste! The lower half of a 4¼″ egg mold shapes the bassinet, and a 3″ round cookie cutter cuts the petals. Lay mold flat on table, dust with cornstarch, and make a recipe of gum paste (page 22).

1. Cut petals one at a time. Roll a small piece of gum paste to about ¹/₁₆″ thick and cut out a circle. Lay on flat part of mold and shape to curve. Cut another petal, lay on a piece of foam toweling, and roll edge on one side with modeling stick 2 to curl it. Immediately place on egg mold, brushing on a little egg white to "glue." Do five more petals the same way until entire egg mold is covered. Prop curled edges of petals with cotton and dry thoroughly.

2. Cut a 1½″ circle from 1″ thick styrofoam for pedestal for the bassinet. Ice with royal icing. When dry, attach bassinet with royal icing. Cut a 4″ x 2″ oval pattern and use it to cut plaque for side of cake. Dry on 12″ curved surface. Pipe script, scrolls and beading with tube 1.

3. One at a time, cut leaves to cover pedestal. Roll out gum paste and cut

Shower the little new-comer with love

a leaf, using Iris Leaf Cutter from Flower Garden set or *Celebrate! IV* pattern. Place on foam toweling and roll over entire leaf with stick 2 to thin and elongate it. Brush pedestal with egg white and attach leaf, propping with cotton to curl up at base. Continue adding leaves until pedestal is covered. Dry thoroughly.

4. Model a little pillow from gum paste, about 1″ x 1½″ wide. Brush back with egg white and place in narrow end of bassinet. When dry, trim with a tube 101 ruffle and a tube 1 flower. Lay purchased baby figure in bassinet. Cut a 3″ square from rolled gum paste and lay over baby. When dry, pipe tube 1 trim.

5. Make tube 33 drop flowers, add tube 2 centers and dry. Bake and fill a two-layer 10″ cake. Swirl boiled icing over cake and pipe a tube 326 leaf border. Attach plaque to cake side on mound of icing. Trim cake with flowers and add tube 66 leaves. This charming cake serves 14.

We'd love a girl...
but a boy would be great!

Bake an easy twin-heart cake that welcomes either a baby boy or girl

into the family. Pipe the dainty royal icing daisies in advance—then the cake is quick to decorate.

1. Pipe about 70 tube 103 daisies in royal icing. Add tube 5 centers and flatten. Dry within curved surface.

2. Bake and fill two 9″ two-layer heart cakes. Ice the cakes individually in buttercream. Divide each curved side of the cakes into eighths and mark about 1″ above base. Cut a 12″ x 18″ oval cake board and cover with foil. Slice about 1″ off curved side of each cake and set them on cake board, cut sides touching.

3. Pipe a tube 16 shell border around base of cakes and a tube 14 border at top. Drop a string guideline from marks and pipe a tube 16 zigzag garland at base. Measure about 1¼″ up from points of garland and drop double tube 3 strings. Pipe a little knot at points of string. Now drop double strings over garlands.

Set violinist from Cherub Concerto set on cakes where the two join. Edge top of cakes with daisies, attaching with dots of icing. Add more daisies to side of cake to conceal area where they join. Serves 20.

Create marvelous little sculptures from icing and wire

Here's a new way to use your decorating skills—turn florists' wire and royal icing into charming little sculptures! Study these directions—soon you'll be creating many little sculptures of your own. Finished figures are shown actual size on pages 30 and 31.

Create Mary's figure

1. Make wire armature for pantaloons. Bend a wire into a upside-down "V" shape, about 2" high. Make a little hook in each end. Make two more upside down "V" shapes, but circle wire around base so they stand alone. These are about 1" high. Hook them on to the larger "V" and use floral tape to secure firmly.

Make the armature for the dress in a similar way, twisting the points of two "V"s together at top. This will form neck. Armature is 2¼" high.

Wire the dress and pantaloon armatures together firmly and add a 2¼" piece of heavy florists' wire for arms. Armature for figure is complete.

2. Cover the armature. Using tube 1, connect the wires with many lines of royal icing until armature is covered. Dry thoroughly, then repeat the procedure.

3. Fill in shapes by piping vertical lines with tube 4, then brushing with a damp brush to form rounded folds. When shapes of dress and pantaloons are defined and dried, pipe tube 3 lines and brush to define apron.

4. Pipe a tube 6 ball on wax paper for front of head. Immediately use a small damp brush to define features. Dry. Secure to neck wire with icing and dry again. Pipe back of head onto front with tube 6 and brush to smooth. Dry.

Curve arms into position. Cover with tube 4 lines and brush to smooth and shape. Figure pipe hands with tube 2. Outline ovals, 1" long for feet. Fill in with tube 6 and brush to shape.

Pipe a little book about ⅝" x ⅜" with tube 2 lines. Brush to smooth. Dry.

5. Finish the figure using tinted icing for paint. See page 30 and pipe hair, eyes, embroidery and polka dots with tube 1. Puffed sleeves are piped with tube 4. Secure book in arm with icing.

Model the baby deer

1. Use stiff florists' wire for the armature. Front and back legs are "V"s joined by a long "V" that curves up for neck and head. Add a second long narrow "V" that curves up in back for rear quarter. Page 31 is a guide for length of wires.

2. Pipe tube 1 lines to connect wires and dry. Use tube 3 to pipe icing on body to give roundness. Brush to define shapes. Figure pipe ears with tube 4 and use brush to hollow. Dry.

3. Use thinned icing to paint figure, and define spots on back. Now cover entire figure with tube 1 short strokes. Use beige for legs, underbody and face, tan for patch on chest, and light brown for rest of coat. Spots are white. Pipe tiny tail.

4. Finish the figure by adding black tube 2 nose and eyes. Use same tube to pipe hooves. Dry thoroughly.

Do the little lamb

1. The armature is similar to the deer's, but simpler as the figure is much smaller. Refer to actual size picture on page 30 for length of wires. Pipe tube 1 lines across back to join and dry.

2. Build up figure with tube 3, brushing to smooth and round. Figure pipe tube 3 ears. Dry thoroughly.

3. Use tube 1s to cover entire body with "wool". Add tube 2 black eyes and brush nose with black icing. Pipe tube 2 hooves. The lamb is ready to follow Mary to school.

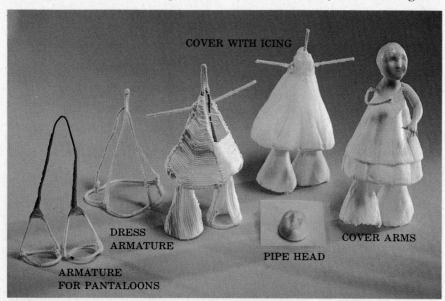

COVER WITH ICING

DRESS ARMATURE

ARMATURE FOR PANTALOONS

PIPE HEAD

COVER ARMS

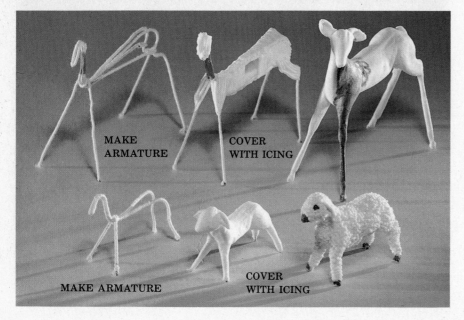

MAKE ARMATURE

COVER WITH ICING

MAKE ARMATURE

COVER WITH ICING

WELCOME TO THE

Sugar Plum Shop

The Sugar Plum Shop has been newly refurbished to display the biggest and best assortment of Birthday Cakes ever decorated! Browse through—you'll find stunning cakes to celebrate anyone's birthday—from toddler, through teen-ager to great-grand-parent.

TWO WORDS SAY IT ALL. Directions for decorating this brilliant birthday cake are on page 70.

A MASTERPIECE LIKE THIS takes planning ahead, so make all trims in advance. The letters on the side of the wagon are Color Flow. The wheels, sculptural designs and plaques are gum paste, and the cupids are plastic, painted with thinned icing. All patterns are in Celebrate! IV Pattern Book.

1. Make a recipe of gum paste (page 22), and tint about half of it gold, the rest red and blue. Use gold gum paste and Baroque Molds to mold side trims. Follow directions in kit and make four Classic Shell designs, six Regalia center shells, four sets of Regalia side plumes and ten tiny Regalia flowers. Dry flat. Turn over and pipe a royal icing "spike" with a star tube on back of each.

Cut four 2¾″ gold circles, ¼″ thick, for wheels. Use pattern to cut eight blue stars. Cut two red plaques for sides of wagon. Dry thoroughly. Brush all gum paste pieces with syrup glaze for a high gloss. (Boil corn syrup for one minute.) Dry. Trim wheels with tube 1 and attach star to each. Trim plaque with tubes 3 and 1 and add gum paste star.

2. Make two sets of Color Flow letters for plaques. Outline patterns with tube 1 and flow in thinned icing. Dry at least 48 hours. Trim large letters with tube 1. Attach to plaques with icing.

3. Mold two dark chocolate elephants in metal elephant mold. First temper chocolate. You will need three pounds for each elephant. Place cut-up chocolate, a cup at a time, into top of double boiler over low heat. Heat to 110°F, stirring occasionally. Remove from heat and let stand until stiff. Now reheat to 90°-92°F, pour into pastry bag fitted with tube 8, and fill mold. Refrigerate until completely hard and remove molds. Cut gum paste costumes from patterns and attach while still wet to elephants with egg white. Attach long gold cord beneath gum paste piece at front of elephant. Brush gum paste pieces when dry with syrup glaze for high gloss. Dry. Trim with tube 1 strings, tassels, beading and fleurs-de-lis.

4. Paint four Angel Musicians and two filigree pedestals with thinned royal icing. Dry, then brush with syrup glaze for high gloss.

5. Figure pipe six jolly clowns in royal icing. Using careful pressure

Continued on page 70

Everybody loves the circus!

A stupendous, gigantic, magnificent cake like this will make happy memories for the delighted birthday child—but it's not just for children. Any circus buff of more mature years will give you the same dazzled smile of pure pleasure when he sees it.

USE YOUR SKILL and imagination when you decorate his birthday cake—he'll appreciate the extra effort that shows how much you care. These cakes will brighten his birthday celebration and provide a glowing memory for many years.

"Love and kisses"

That's the translation of the message on this CB cake. He'll return the same to you.

1. Cookies provide the detail on the CB receiver and microphone. Cut a rectangular cookie 6″ × 4″ for the top of the receiver and one 2″ × 1¼″ for the microphone. Groove the cookies with the edge of a ruler. Cut two 1⅜″ round cookies, one 1¾″ and one 1″ in diameter. Cut three tiny heart cookies. Use your favorite recipe or the one on page 147. After baking, paint the cookies with thinned royal icing, and assemble the round cookies as picture shows. Trim the 1¾″ cookie with tube 1.

2. Bake and fill a 10″ two-layer round cake. Chill an 8″ single-layer square cake. Cut a 5″ × 7″ rectangle from it for receiver. Cut a 3½″ × 2½″ × 1″ slice for microphone and taper the narrow end. Ice all, and assemble on foil-covered cake board.

3. Edge receiver with tube 5 balls. Pipe a line on side with same tube. Attach cookie dials with icing and secure large rectangular cookie on top of receiver.

Pipe tube 10 ball border at base of round cake. Edge top with tube 7 balls. Pipe message with tube 5. Use tube 8 to pipe the spiraled cord. Attach small rectangular cookie to microphone and set microphone on cake board, securing with mound of icing. Push tall tapers into cake behind receiver. Serves about 21.

A basket of joy . . .

a barrel of love and a bucket of sunshine is the birthday wish for father!

1. Bake cookie trims first. Use alphabet cutters for "JOY" and "DAD." Bake letters for "JOY" on toothpicks so picks can be pushed into cake. Cut about a dozen 1″ heart cookies. Bake four or five of them on toothpicks. You'll also need a 2¼″ round cookie, trimmed at base, for sun and several little people cut with small Gingerbread cutters.

After baking, outline clothing areas on people with tube 1 and royal icing. Flow in areas with thinned icing and pipe details with tube 1. Outline let-

Decorate
a special cake
for a
special man

46

ters and hearts with tube 2 and fill in with thinned icing. Pipe face on cookie sun with tube 2 and edge with tube 14 icing "rays".

2. Bake, fill and ice a two-layer 9″ × 13″ sheet cake. Set on cake board. Bake a Little Loafer for the basket and three small Wonder Mold cakes for the barrel and bucket.

Pipe handle for basket with tube 47 and royal icing over bottom of Little Loafer pan. Dry. Ice the cake thinly, then cover sides with tube 46 basket weave. Add zigzag border with tube 13. Attach handle to basket on mounds of icing. Insert toothpicked letters into basket.

Make barrel by stacking two Wonder Mold cakes, large ends together. Trim off smaller ends, pipe "staves" with tube 48, then add tube 46 "hoops". Add toothpicked heart cookies in top of barrel.

Trim and taper a Wonder Mold cake to bucket shape. Pipe handle over a 3″ fruit can and dry. Ice cake, attach handle and set sun cookie in position.

3. Pipe tube 19 shell border at base of sheet cake and a tube 17 border at top. Pipe message with tube 2. Attach heart, people and alphabet cookies on sides of cake with mounds of icing. Set the basket, barrel and bucket cakes on top and add tall tapers. Light them before you lead Dad in for a sweet surprise! Serves about 28.

Oak leaves for your man

1. Make marzipan (recipe, page 23). Divide half the batch into three parts and tint yellow, gold and scarlet. From the remaining half-batch, tint one portion light brown and one green. Roll out 1/16″ thick and cut leaves using Celebrate! IV pattern or Flower Garden cutter. Dry within a curved surface, brush with corn syrup and dry. Paint veins with copper food color.

Model acorns about ½″ in diameter and ¾″ long. Model green "caps" about ½″ x ½″ and attach with egg white. Press in lines on "caps". Dry. Brush with corn syrup and dry.

2. Bake a two-layer 9″ oval tier and a 9″ x 13″ x 3″ tier. Fill and ice with buttercream and assemble on foil-covered board. Write tube 2 message on 9″ x 13″ tier. Pipe tube 19 shells around base of this tier and tube 16 shells around top. Pipe tube 16 shells around base of oval tier and tube 15 shells around top.

3. Attach acorns and leaves with icing. Position Push-In Candle Holders around oval tier. Serves 36.

Twenty-one!

1. Make 72 tube 103 royal icing daisies in pink, yellow and red. Add tube 5 centers and dry within a curved surface. Mount half on wires.

2. Outline "21" pattern from Celebrate! IV Pattern Book with tube 2 and fill in with Color Flow icing. When dry, trim with tube 2 dots.

3. Paint three Heart Bowls with three coats of thinned royal icing. Ice three styrofoam ball halves. Anchor in bowls with icing. Insert seven slender tapers in each and add wired daisies.

4. Bake two 11″ x 15″ layers and two 6″ round layers. Fill and ice with buttercream. Assemble on foil-covered board, placing 6″ tier near back of bottom tier. Pipe bottom border with tube 19 stars, piping three tube 19 upright shells topped with a star at each corner.

Drop a string down front of bottom tier as garland guide line. From the edge of string, pipe tube 16 stars around top of tier and down corners. Pipe tube 2 birthday message. Attach daisies with icing along guide line. Pipe tube 16 stars for top and bottom borders on 6″ tier. Attach numerals with dots of icing.

5. Anchor bowls with icing. Attach daisies around bowls. Serves 40.

Glorious blazing cakes for important birthdays

Every birthday is a red letter day, but there are some important milestones in a loved one's life that you want to make especially memorable. Do it with a stunning cake that says "You're special!"

Make it for your man

HERE'S A TRIO of cakes directed toward masculine interests and colored in hearty tones. Decorate one for your favorite man—husband, father, son, or just someone very special. He'll love it—and you! Each starts with an easy-to-serve 9″ x 13″ sheet cake.

Does he jog every morning?

Give him a cake disguised as a warm-up suit! Perhaps his present could be a real suit.

1. Bake a 9″ x 13″ x 2″ high sheet cake. Chill cake, ice thickly and set on foil-covered board. Pat all over with clean damp sponge for stucco effect.

2. With a toothpick, draw a line down center of cake from top to bottom. On top edge of cake, make a mark 2″ from either side of center line. Make a mark on center line 4½″ down from top. Connect this mark with the two marks on top edge of cake. This forms the "Y" shape that describes V-neck and zipper.

On right side of cake, make a mark 1½″ from bottom and another 6½″ from bottom. These two marks represent the width of the sleeve. Extend them to base of cake, and then across center line on top to mark the folded sleeve. Fill in this area with thick coat of icing applied with a spatula. Pat with damp sponge.

3. Pipe rows of tube 16 stars at top edge of cake to simulate stripes. Alternate gold and brown stars. Do the same at top edge of sleeve. Do the zipper with two tube 46 lines, one on either side of center line.

4. Pipe "ribbing" with tube 16 zig-zag. First do back edge of neck, then front of V-neck, following the marked lines and making it about 1″ wide. Pipe ribbed cuff on sleeve, making it about 1¾″ wide. Pipe zipper pull with tube 8. Pipe a tube 18 star border at base of cake.

Cut a little card from colored paper and pipe script with tube 1. Glue the card to a tall taper and insert in cake. Serves 24.

Is he a man about town?

Then bake him a dress shirt, complete with ruffles and colorful bow tie!

1. Make the collar and tie from gum paste, using *Celebrate! IV* patterns. Trace collar pattern twice on light cardboard. Fold and tape one cardboard pattern to shape of collar. This will serve as a form to dry the collar on. Tint gum paste (recipe page 22) roll out about 1/16" thick on surface dusted with cornstarch and cut collar. Dust form with cornstarch and drape collar over it to dry. Roll out a small piece of gum paste and cut tie. Pleat tie in center. Cut a strip of gum paste about ¾" x 3". Brush one side with egg white and wrap around center of tie. Lay tie on collar to dry thoroughly.

2. Ice a chilled 9" x 13" x 2" cake very smoothly with buttercream. Mark a toothpick line down center and one on either side of it about 1½" away. Mark position of sleeve just as for warm-up jacket. Outline sleeve with tube 3 and fill in second layer of icing with a spatula. Smooth with damp brush. Outline cuff with tube 3.

3. Place dried collar on cake and mark its position lightly. Set aside. Now starting at outside marked line, pipe a tube 103 ruffle on cake from collar mark to base of cake. Add a second ruffle. Pipe two ruffles on opposite side of cake, following marked line. Pipe two tube 47 lines on inner edges of double ruffles. Pipe a tube 2B line in center.

4. Edge cuff with a tube 103 ruffle. Add tube 10 buttons and flatten with damp fingertip. Pipe a tube 6 ball border at base of cake. Attach collar and tie with dots of icing. Pipe message on a card with tube 1 and glue to taper. Insert taper in cake and call the birthday boy. Serves 24.

Is he a serious skier?

He'll love this ski sweater cake! Diamond-shaped cookie cutters form the design to fill in with easy stars.

1. Cover a 9" x 13" x 2" cake with a thin coat of chocolate buttercream. Mark a line 4" down from top of cake and another 8¾" down. This defines horizontal stripe. Mark center line on stripe. Mark sleeve area just as for warm-up jacket. Outline with tube 3 and fill in with thick layer of icing.

Mark ribbed cuff and 3¾" stripe on sleeve. Mark a semi-circle on top of cake to define neck ribbing.

2. Use 3⅛" Diamond cutter to mark three large diamonds on stripe. Mark inner areas with smaller cutter. Press 1¼" cutter into icing to make designs between large diamonds and on sides of cake. Use 1¾" and 1¼" diamond cutters to mark design on sleeve stripe.

3. Use tube 17 for all decorating. Outline stripes with two contrasting rows of stars. Make third stripe, using alternating white and chocolate stars. Pipe colored diamond design with stars. Fill in rest of stripe with white stars.

4. Pipe zigzag at cuff and neck. Now fill in entire sweater with chocolate stars. Write message on card with tube 1, glue to taper and insert into cake. Serves 24.

A luscious layer cake in his favorite flavor

He'll never believe how quickly you decorated this handsome cake!

1. Bake and fill a two-layer cake. (He probably prefers chocolate.) Ice top in vanilla, sides in chocolate buttercream. Press cake-top Pattern Press on top to transfer design. Outline the design with tube 3, let set, then fill in with tinted piping gel for a glittery effect. Pipe top and bottom shell borders with tube 16.

2. Divide cake into twelfths, measure about 1½" up from base and mark. Drop strings from mark to mark with tube 2. Add two more sets of strings below first. Add dots at points of string. Push in the tapers and serve to 14.

Quick & Pretty

51

Decorate a cake to suit her personality

Here is a feminine threesome of birthday cakes decorated with the lady's tastes in mind. Vary them by using her favorite colors. She'll love her cake—and you for being so thoughtful. Just remember — every girl of any age loves flowers!

Does she like dainty things?
Present her with Rose Monogram

If she likes lacy lingerie, embroidered linens and flowery china this is the cake for her.

1. Pipe about 20 royal icing roses in advance with tube 103. Dry and mount on wire stems. Pipe tube 66 leaves on wires. Dry, then surround roses with leaves and tape into four small clusters.

2. The monogram is piped on a gum paste circle. See page 22 for recipe and guidelines. Roll out a little gum paste 1/16″ thick and cut with a 3″ cookie cutter. Dry on a 10″ curve. Using *Celebrate! IV* patterns, transfer her initials to circle. Making tiny strokes with tube 1, outline initials and fill in with horizontal lines. Edge circle with tube 2 beading. Dry.

3. Bake a two-layer oval cake. Fill, ice and place on cake board. Pipe tube 4 bottom ball border and tube 2 top border. Attach gum paste circle with dots of icing. "Embroider" dot flowers and leaves around it with tube 1. Starting below embroidery, drop tube 2 strings around cake. Pipe tube 1 dot flowers and leaves at point of string and below it.

4. Push four Flower Spikes into top of cake. Insert tall tapers in center, then fill Flower Spikes with rose clusters, securing in place with icing. Serves twelve.

Is she a sophisticate?
Abstract Tulip is for her

If she likes chrome and glass, modern paintings and foreign foods, decorate her cake with this stylized flower design in gleaming piping gel.

1. Bake a two-layer 12″ petal cake. Fill and ice, then place on cake board or tray. Transfer *Celebrate! IV* pattern to cake top. Outline with tube 3, let set, then fill in with piping gel.

2. Pipe a double line with tube 6 around base of cake. At inner points of each "petal", pipe a tailored fleur-de-lis with same tube. Edge top of cake with tube 3 bulb border. Insert Push-In Candle Holders in cake side and add birthday candles. Finish each holder with a tube 14 star. Serves 26.

Does she love home and garden?
Drape wisteria on her cake

If she makes new plants from cuttings, drapes shining windows with crisp white curtains, and grows prize-winning flowers, enchant her with this latticed wisteria cake.

1. Make four sprays of wisteria, as explained below. You'll enjoy the showy effect of this flower—newly piped in icing.

2. Tape *Celebrate! IV* pattern to curved surface and cover with wax paper. You will need seven lattice pieces made on a 10″ curve and four made on a 6″ curve. Pipe lattice with tube 44 within oval and outline with tube 3. Edge with tube 3 beading. Use the same oval pattern to cut a gum paste plaque. (See recipe and guidelines, page 22.) Dry plaque on 10″ curve. Edge with tube 3 beading. Pipe tube 2 message. If you prefer, make plaque with Color Flow.

3. Bake 10″ x 4″ and 6″ x 3″ round, two-layer tiers. Fill, ice and assemble on cake stand. Pipe tube 7 balls around base of 10″ tier and tube 5 balls around top. On top and bottom edges of 6″ tier, pipe tube 5 balls. Attach gum paste and lattice ovals to sides of tiers with dots of icing.

4. Push in tapers on top tier. Lay a wisteria spray in front of them, attaching with icing. Lay three wisteria sprays on base tier. Serves 20.

How to pipe wisteria

This old-fashioned flower makes a lovely feminine cake trim. Here's how to create it in violet royal icing.

1. Using tube 401 and number 7 flower nail, pipe the back of the flower. Pinch to triangular shape. Use deeper violet icing to pipe the little curved petal. When dry, paint pollen with brush and thinned yellow icing.

2. Pipe calyxes with tube 3 on squares of wax paper. Insert fine florists' wire stems in each and set upright in styrofoam to dry. Tape about 20 into triangular cluster.

3. Pipe leaves on wax paper directly on florists' wire stems. Tape into groups of five.

4. Pipe tube 6 buds on calyxes at tip of cluster and attach dried flowers to remaining calyxes with dots of icing. Add groups of leaves and tape together into completed sprays.

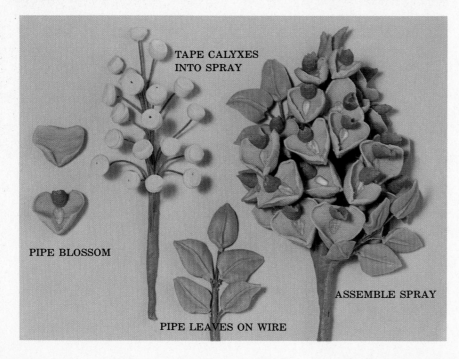

TAPE CALYXES INTO SPRAY

PIPE BLOSSOM

PIPE LEAVES ON WIRE

ASSEMBLE SPRAY

Quick & Pretty

LAVISH HER CAKE with a lot of love, but very little time. Pretty pastel icing and basic techniques can turn out a cake just as appealing as one that took many hours to decorate.

Little gift cakes

Present a tray of petits fours dressed up like birthday presents at her party. The girls will love them.

1. Using your favorite sponge cake or jelly roll recipe, bake a cake in an 11" × 17" pan. Cut the cake into two layers, each 11" × 8½" and fill the layers with jam or Snow-white Buttercream. (Recipe, page 16.) Cut into rectangles about 2" × 3" and ice with buttercream. Let the icing set a little, then place the cakes on a wire rack over a cookie sheet. Make a recipe of Quick Fondant (page 13) and pour the fondant over, touching up bare spots with a spatula. Let the fondant harden.

2. Tie ribbons around the cakes with tube 44 and add tube 101 bows. Trim with drop flowers or any other small flowers you may have made in advance and stored. Insert Crystal Clear candle holders and add colored birthday candles.

The soft shine of the fondant sets off the pastel trims and the little cakes present a very festive picture.

A love-knot cake

Tie a sheet cake with blue bows and edge it with a feminine ruffle.

1. Pipe wild roses with tube 104 and center with tube 1 stamens. If you are using buttercream, air-dry or freeze the flowers. If the flowers are piped with royal icing, dry thoroughly before placing on cake.

2. Bake a 9" × 13" × 3" cake. Ice smoothly with buttercream. Pipe a tube 10 bulb border at base and a tube 6 top border. Pipe the birthday message with tube 2, and use the same tube for curving stems. Pipe a tube 124 ruffle over the base border and edge with tube 4 beading.

3. Pipe flowing tube 104 bows on top and corners of cake. Pipe a tube 10 "knot." Pipe mounds of icing at ends of stems and position flowers. Add tube 67 leaves. Insert candles in Crystal Clear holders. Serve to 24.

A circle of daisies . . .

grow on the sides of this sunny cake. Just one tube, tube 17, does all the decorating.

Quick & Pretty cakes for ladies

1. Bake a 10″ two-layer cake, fill and ice in buttercream. Divide cake side into eighths and mark on top edge. Pull a stem down from top to base. Pipe a leaf on either side of stem.

2. Mark center of cake top and pipe a twelve-petaled daisy. Each petal is an elongated shell. Center with a rosette. Pipe eight daisies around side of cake, giving each ten petals. Center with rosettes. Finish with a star border at base. All that's left to do is light the candle! Serves 14.

Heart flower

A charming little cake, topped with a ring of hearts. Use cookie cutters as pattern presses to keep the piping neat and even.

1. Bake and fill a two-layer 8″ square cake. Ice sides green, top white. Pipe ball borders, tube 10 at base, tube 5 at top of cake.

2. Press a 4″ round cookie cutter on top of cake. Use a 1″ heart cutter to mark twelve hearts around it. Pipe birthday message with tube 2 in center of circle. Now figure pipe the hearts with tube 12. Pipe a tube 6 ball between each. Mark center of each side of tier and on corners. Mark hearts with cutter and pipe with tube 12. Center with tube 6. Insert candles in Crystal Clear holders and push into cake. Serves twelve.

Happy Birthday!

Quick & Pretty

Birthday cakes for your favorite couple

MOM AND DAD will love these cheery cakes—and you'll enjoy showing your love and esteem by decorating them. Of course, they're just as appropriate for any special man or lady. Read these pages to discover time-saving decorating techniques that give them an impressive look.

Heartfelt greetings to Mom

Show her how much you love her by presenting her with this cake with a brilliant piping gel design on top.

1. Bake a 9″ two-layer heart cake. Transfer *Celebrate! IV* pattern to top of cake. Mix piping gel with an equal amount of royal icing and outline design with tube 2. This mixture gives a glossy look to the outline. Let set. Mix piping gel with an equal amount of water, tint, put in parchment cone with tip cut and fill in design.

2. Pipe tube 17 reverse shell borders at top and bottom of cake. Use a 2½″ heart cutter to press designs on side of cake. Outline designs with tube 16 swirls. Add Push-In Candle Holders, insert candles and you're ready for the party! Serves twelve.

Happy 39th, Dad!

Dad won't mind a gentle joke when it's accompanied by a lot of love and a birthday cake in his favorite flavor.

1. Bake and fill a two-layer oval cake. Ice smoothly, then transfer *Celebrate! IV* pattern to cake top. Outline with a mixture of half piping gel and half royal icing using tube 3. Do lettering with same mixture and tube.

2. Warm a little quick fondant (page 13), tint and put in cone with cut tip. Fill in outlined numbers. Add base bulb border with tube 8, top border with tube 6. Insert candles in Push-In Candle Holders and call Dad. Serves twelve.

A regal scroll for Father

Baroque molds done in gum paste

Quick & Pretty

give a very important look to an otherwise simple cake.

1. Make gum paste recipe (page 22), tint golden and mold six Scrolls. Follow directions that come with the Baroque Mold set. Dry on flat surface. When dry, pipe tube 1s message on all scrolls with royal icing and add a little tube 2 heart on four scrolls. Turn the four side scrolls over and pipe two royal icing spikes on back of each with tube 5. Cement toothpicks to back of scrolls for top of cake with royal icing.

2. Bake, fill and ice a two-layer 8″ square cake. Make a 7″ semi-circle pattern and transfer to side of cake. Transfer *Celebrate! IV* pattern to top of cake. Fill in designs with tube 16 stars. Insert taper in center of cake and push in scroll designs on either side of it. Pipe mounds of icing on sides of cake and push in four side scrolls. This handsome cake serves twelve.

Daisies and shells for Mother

See how Baroque Classic Shells give a professional finish to this little cake! Mother will love it.

1. Make two dozen royal icing daisies with tube 103. Add tube 5 centers and flatten with fingertip. Dry within curved surface. Pipe tube 66 leaves on wires. Mount daisies on wire stems. Tape into two clusters with floral tape.

2. Mold a Classic Shell design in gum paste (recipe, page 22), following directions that come with the Baroque set. Dust outside of oval pan with cornstarch and dry design against narrow end of pan so shell flares out at bottom and rests on table. Mold five more shells and dry the same way. When dry, pipe a royal icing tube 5 spike on back of four shells.

3. Bake, fill and ice a two-layer oval cake. Pipe message on side with tube 2. Edge with tube 5 bulb borders. Push in shell design on mound of icing on base of cake at each narrow curved end. Add upside-down shell designs just above them.

Push a taper into center of cake and a Flower Spike on either side. Set a shell design on both sides of taper, securing each with icing and a toothpick. Arrange daisy clusters in Flower Spikes. Serves twelve.

Celebrations for the young set

BIRTHDAYS MEAN SO MUCH when the years they mark are few. Lavish your skill, imagination and love on the birthday cakes you decorate for little children. You'll be rewarded by the expressions of pure delight.

Trim a cake with teddy bears

It's easy to figure pipe these cute little bears with the help of royal icing and *Celebrate! IV* patterns.

1. Tape patterns for four standing bears on a 10″ curved surface, two seated bears on a 6″ curve, and one seated bear on a flat surface. Tape wax paper smoothly over patterns. Pipe chubby bodies with tube 12 and heavy pressure. Tuck same tube into body and pipe legs with lighter pressure. Mound up head. Use tube 5 to pipe ears and muzzle. Add pink trim with tube 4. When dry, attach a tiny ribbon bow with icing.

When piping seated bears, omit piping the lower legs until rest of bear is thoroughly dry. Then prop body upright and pipe lower legs. Dry again.

Turn four standing bears over and pipe tube 5 spikes on backs.

Tape heart pattern to a 6″ curve, tape wax paper over and outline with Color Flow icing. Fill in with thinned icing. When thoroughly dry, use tube 2 to pipe name and beading.

2. Bake 10″ × 4″ and 6″ × 3″ round tiers. Fill, ice and assemble on cake board. Circle the base of the 10″ tier with tube 10 balls. Pipe the top border of the tier with tube 7 balls. Pipe tube 6 ball borders on 6″ tier.

3. Write birthday message with tube 2. Attach the Color Flow heart with dots of icing. Push spikes on standing bears into cake side on mounds of icing. Push taper into top of cake. Secure the seated bears. Serves 20.

Flying high!

1. Tape *Celebrate! IV* patterns for the large kite, children and dogs to 10″ curves and smaller kites to 8″ curves. Tape wax paper over. Outline with tube 1 and Color Flow icing. Let set and flow in thinned icing. Dry about 48 hours. Pipe details on the figures with tube 1. Attach a 6″ length of stiff florists' wire to the back of the large kite with royal icing. Let wire extend 3″ from bottom of kite. Make kite tails by tying small pieces of ¼″ wide ribbon around lengths of thin gold cord. Use the same cord for the kite strings. Attach to the backs of the kites with dots of icing.

2. Bake 10″ × 4″ and 6″ × 3″ round tiers. Fill, ice and assemble on cake board using a 6″ round separator plate and four Crystal Clear pillars.

3. Pipe tube 6 balls around the base of each pillar. Circle the top of the 10″ tier with tube 6 balls. On the 6″ tier, pipe tube 6 ball borders.

4. Pipe tube 2 "grass" around the bottom of the 10″ tier. Add tube 8 ball border. Attach the children and dogs to the side of the tier with dots of icing. Secure the small kites to the side of the 6″ tier and push the wire on the large kite into the top of the tier through to plate. Attach kite strings to the hands of the children with dots of icing. Add candles in Crystal Clear holders. Serves 20.

A bunny in a hat? It's magic

1. Start with three 6″ layers. Fill and stack the layers and brush with apricot glaze. (Heat one cup of apricot preserves to boiling and strain.)

2. Make a recipe of marzipan (page 23) and tint. Form about half of it into a long cylinder and roll out to ¼″ thickness to a rough rectangle about 19″ × 7″. Trim one long side straight. Place the cake on it, side down, and roll to cover. Secure seam by brushing with a little egg white. Trim

lower edge and set upright on a 14″ cake board. Ice top of cake.

3. Cut a 9½″ circle from stiff cardboard and cut 5″ circle from center as support for brim. Make pattern for brim by drawing a 10″ circle with a 5″ circle cut from center. Roll marzipan ¼″ thick and cut brim. Lay on cardboard support, attaching with a little egg white. Attach brim to top of cake with icing.

4. Cut flowers from marzipan using daisy and violet cutters and attach to hat with egg white. Cut candle holders with daisy cutter, cut holes in center with tube 12. Dip candles in egg white and set in holes. Dry. Cut a few more flowers and attach to toothpicks with egg white.

5. Using *Celebrate! IV* pattern, cut ears from light cardboard. Model a half-ball from marzipan, 2¼″ in diameter. Cut in half, brush cut sides with egg white, insert ears and put back together. Ice inside of ears with pink icing. Set head on cake and cover with tube 14 stars, over-piping chubby cheeks. Add tube 3 eyes and nose. Pipe a mound of icing on brim on either side of head. Cover with stars for paws. Push toothpicked flowers into cake and set candles on board. This magic trick serves twelve.

Quick & Pretty

Yes, it's Big Bird!*

Here's your friend from Sesame Street—he'll be the most popular guest at the party!

1. Bake a cake in the Big Bird pan and cool completely. Mound icing on beak and smooth with spatula. Mound more icing above eyes and on sides of head.

2. Outline the beak with tube 3, then fill in with tube 14 stars. Pipe protruding eyes with tube 1A and let icing set. Pipe eyelids with tube 14 stars and add a tube 102 ribbon of icing at edge of eyelid. Pipe tube 9 pupil and flatten with a damp fingertip. When dry, glaze with corn syrup.

3. Flow in thinned royal icing for mouth and when set, pipe a tube 102 tongue with light pressure.

4. Pipe a 401 feather on the ends of five 6″ lengths of thin white cloth-covered florists' wire. Stick them into a piece of styrofoam to dry. Then pipe short tube 401 feathers around beak and eyes, making longer feathers on sides of face and top of head. While piping feathers, keep turning tube so they are not all facing the same direction. Pipe a second layer of long feathers on sides of face and top of head. Insert wired feathers into top of head. If you like, you can bake the Count, Cookie Monster, Oscar, and Ernie and Bert too!*

A cuddly teddy bear

Bake this stout little fellow in an Egg pan, a Ball Pan, four Little Loafers and a cupcake! Diagram shows how.

6″ ball cake trimmed at base. Attach cupcake with toothpicks

Dowel rods secure head

Trim egg cake for body
Toothpicks between layers

Trim Little Loafers for upper legs. Secure with picks

1. Outline bib area, eyes, nose and mouth with tube 3. Figure pipe the ears on toothpicks in royal icing, letting picks extend from ears. When dry, stick into head. Cover body and legs with tube 18 stars, head with tube 16 stars.

2. Figure pipe eyes and nose with tube 10, flatten with fingertip. Over-pipe mouth with same tube. Use tube 104 to pipe ruffle around bib and to tie a big red bow. Glaze eyes and nose with syrup glaze. Teddy serves about 29 guests.

Happy birthday, little friend

Bake these four little playmates in Mini Rag Doll pans and pipe a guest's name on each of their T shirts. One cake mix bakes them all. Perhaps you'd better decorate a sheet cake too—the guests will insist on taking their playmates home.

1. Chill the cakes after baking, then trim off skirt areas for boy figures. Outline all areas and pipe names and features with tube 2. For boy figures, cover faces with tube 13 stars and do rest of figure with tube 14 stars.

Pipe the face on the girl figures with tube 13. Pipe shoes and legs with tube 14, then add flared skirt with tube 127D. Cover T shirt and arms with tube 14 stars.

2. Now over-pipe mouth, eyes and names with tube 2 and pipe hair with same tube. Put candles in Crystal Clear holders and insert in hands.

Sweet little cakes for twins

If you're not lucky enough to have twins, one of these cakes will be very well received at a toddler's birthday.

1. Pipe royal icing roses with tube 127 just as shown on page 20, but omit step 2. Insert birthday candles and set aside to dry.

2. Bake two-layer cakes in 6½″ Mini-Tier pans. Fill and ice. Pipe tube 16 borders at top and bottom.

3. Divide cake into sixths and mark at top. Pipe triple tube 20 shells at five of the marks. Pipe name on side of cake with tube 3, centering in space between shells. Over-pipe with tube 13 stars. Now pipe double strings from shell to shell, swinging down below name. Pipe a tube 13 rosette where strings meet. Serve each cake to six.

Birthday joys for girls and boys

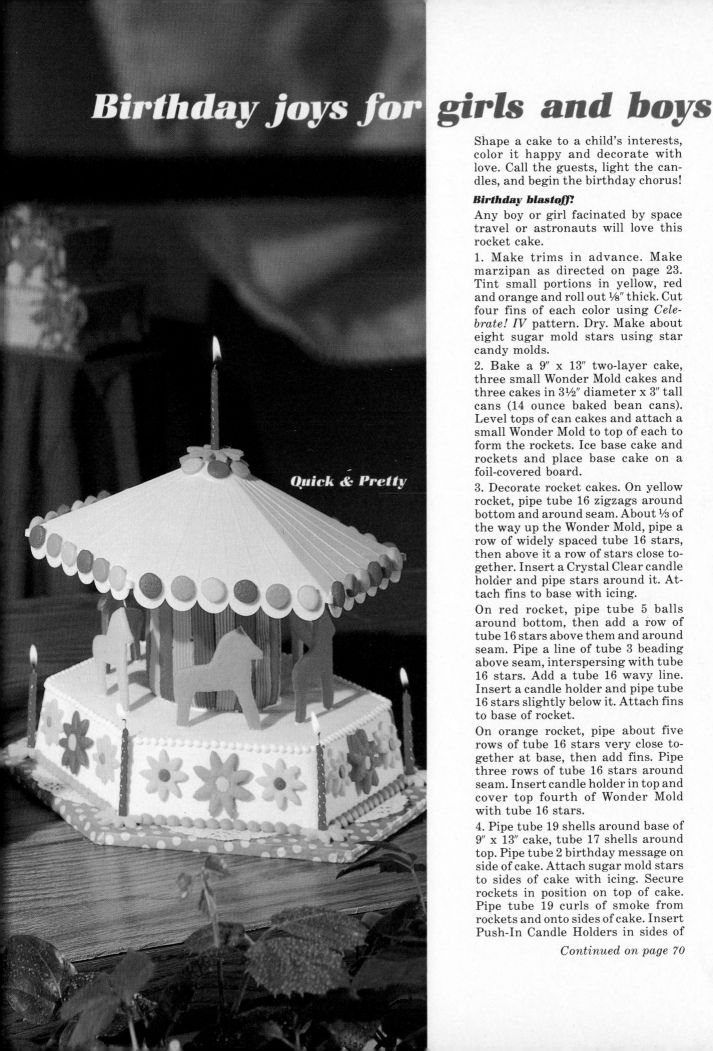

Quick & Pretty

Shape a cake to a child's interests, color it happy and decorate with love. Call the guests, light the candles, and begin the birthday chorus!

Birthday blastoff!

Any boy or girl facinated by space travel or astronauts will love this rocket cake.

1. Make trims in advance. Make marzipan as directed on page 23. Tint small portions in yellow, red and orange and roll out ⅛" thick. Cut four fins of each color using *Celebrate! IV* pattern. Dry. Make about eight sugar mold stars using star candy molds.

2. Bake a 9" x 13" two-layer cake, three small Wonder Mold cakes and three cakes in 3½" diameter x 3" tall cans (14 ounce baked bean cans). Level tops of can cakes and attach a small Wonder Mold to top of each to form the rockets. Ice base cake and rockets and place base cake on a foil-covered board.

3. Decorate rocket cakes. On yellow rocket, pipe tube 16 zigzags around bottom and around seam. About ⅓ of the way up the Wonder Mold, pipe a row of widely spaced tube 16 stars, then above it a row of stars close together. Insert a Crystal Clear candle holder and pipe stars around it. Attach fins to base with icing.

On red rocket, pipe tube 5 balls around bottom, then add a row of tube 16 stars above them and around seam. Pipe a line of tube 3 beading above seam, interspersing with tube 16 stars. Add a tube 16 wavy line. Insert a candle holder and pipe tube 16 stars slightly below it. Attach fins to base of rocket.

On orange rocket, pipe about five rows of tube 16 stars very close together at base, then add fins. Pipe three rows of tube 16 stars around seam. Insert candle holder in top and cover top fourth of Wonder Mold with tube 16 stars.

4. Pipe tube 19 shells around base of 9" x 13" cake, tube 17 shells around top. Pipe tube 2 birthday message on side of cake. Attach sugar mold stars to sides of cake with icing. Secure rockets in position on top of cake. Pipe tube 19 curls of smoke from rockets and onto sides of cake. Insert Push-In Candle Holders in sides of

Continued on page 70

Sugar Plum Shop

HERE'S A FRESH EASY WAY to create dramatic Color Flow effects on cakes without any of the difficulty that sometimes occurs when the Color Flow pieces are rather large and need strength to stand upright.

We enlisted the aid of gum paste (recipe, page 22), that magic substance, when we decorated these charming tableaux cakes. First the pattern pieces (all in Celebrate! IV Pattern Book) were cut from rolled out gum paste, ⅛" thick, with a sharp knife. After drying, the pattern was transferred to the gum paste piece by tracing with a sharp pencil. Then the pattern was outlined and filled in directly on the gum paste shapes. Popsicle sticks were attached to the back of the designs with royal icing, dried and pushed into the cake to achieve the three-dimensional effect. The gum paste backing gives each piece strength and stability and eliminates the need for turning the dried Color Flow design over and reflowing the back. This often leads to colors bleeding.

You can use the same method with any simple design, whether upright or on the cake surface. Color Flow pieces made in this way are also easy to lift off the cake before serving.

Stage Peter's garden adventure

Here Peter is discovered in Mr. McGregor's garden, happily chewing on a crisp tasty carrot. For a quiet time before the spectacular cake is unveiled, read Beatrix Potter's famous story to the little party guests.

1. Cut Peter from beige gum paste, cabbages and bush from green gum paste and the fence pieces from white. Outline Peter with tube 1, and

flow in with thinned icing. When dry, add features and trim with tube 2. Pipe tube 3 radish and carrot, add tube 65s and tube 1 leaves. Attach popsicle stick to back.

Outline cabbages and bush with tube 3 and flow in. When dry, pipe tube 104 petals on cabbages. Attach popsicle stick to back of each. Fence is not iced. Assemble with royal icing, and attach two sticks to back.

2. Outline letters of the birthday child's name with tube 1 and flow in thinned icing. Pipe tube 33 and 34 drop flowers with tube 2 centers. Mount on wires. Pipe tube 66 leaves on wires. Dry. Tape leaves to flowers with floral tape.

3. Bake and fill an 8″ two-layer square cake. Place on serving plate. Ice sides smoothly. Ice top and pat with a clean, damp sponge for stucco effect. Pipe tube 8 bottom ball border and tube 6 top ball border. Pipe tube 1 birthday message and attach Color Flow name with icing. Attach flowers and leaves to one corner.

4. Beginning at rear of cake top, insert sticks on bush into cake. Insert a few flowers and leaves in front of bush. Add fence, then more flowers and leaves. Push cabbages into cake, then add Peter. Place a few carrots in front of him. Insert Push-In Candle Holders into sides of cake. Serve to twelve happy party guests.

Red Riding Hood goes walking

Delight a little girl on her birthday with this "pop-up" scene from one of her favorite fairy tales.

1. Figure and background are done just as described above. Cut bushes and trees from green gum paste, Riding Hood from beige. Outline her

Continued on page 70

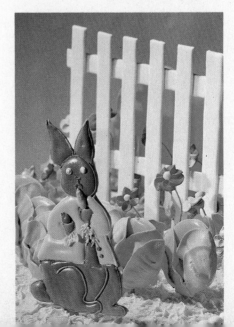

"I'd like to be a ballet dancer . . .
when I grow up." Almost every little girl is fascinated by the ballet. Top her cake with a figurine she'll keep as a treasured memento.

1. Make Color Flow letters. Tape _Celebrate! IV_ patterns to stiff board, tape wax paper over and outline with tube 1 and Color Flow icing. Thin icing and flow in areas. Pipe drop flowers with tube 33 and add tube 2 centers. Dry all thoroughly.

2. Bake, fill and ice the two-layer tiers—12″ round and 9″ petal. Assemble on cake board, inserting dowel rods in round cake for support.

3. Edge top and bottom of 12″ tier with tube 16 shells. Pipe the "C"-shaped swirls at base with tube 17 and pipe more swirls on top of tier. Pipe five wavy parallel lines around side of tier with tube 1. Attach letters with little mounds of icing.

4. Pipe a tube 16 shell border on base of petal tier. Pipe tube 17 swirls on top edge. Put candles in Push-In Candle Holders and insert in cake. Attach drop flowers to candle holders and lower tier with icing. Add tube 66 leaves. Set Dancing Ballerina figure on cake top. Serves 30.

Make it a slumber party
Little marzipan figures enact the bed-time activity.

1. Each of the little marzipan figures is modeled in a similar way. (Marzipan recipe, page 23.) Legs start with cylinders about 3½″ long, bodies are bell-shapes about 1½″ to 2″ high, arms are 2½″ cylinders with mitten-shaped hands added. Heads are balls, ⅞″ in diameter. Model out-size feet so figures can stand alone. Make the pillows about 1½″ square.

Join the parts with egg white and insert half-toothpicks to secure heads to bodies. Pipe the hair and features with tube 2 and add collars, ruffles and bows with tube 101. Paint red stripes on night shirt with food color. Dry figures 48 hours.

2. Bake, fill and ice a 10″ square, two-layer cake. Set on 12″ × 14″ cake board, allowing room at front for figures. Pipe message with tube 2. Pipe tube 6 ball border at base and trim with tube 3 dots. Pipe top border with tube 3. Add candles in Crystal Clear holders and set figures on cake. Serves 20 guests.

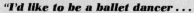

Pink cakes, pretty cakes

Ice cream cones!

Everybody gets an ice cream cone with their serving of cake.

1. Tape *Celebrate! IV* patterns to small Flower Formers and tape wax paper over. Pipe the close lattice with tube 2, and dry.

2. Bake, fill and ice a 10″ two-layer round cake. Set on cake board. Divide cake side into fourteenths and mark just above base. At each mark pipe tube 17 shells in flower shapes. Pipe a rosette between each flower, and garnish with half a candied cherry. Pipe tube 2 message on top of cake, then pipe tube 16 shell border.

3. Attach cones with icing. Use tube 1A to fill with boiled icing or marshmallow creme. Add a cherry to each and push in tapers. Serves 14.

A big, beautiful rag doll

Tots and teen-agers will love her!

1. Bake the cakes to build the doll. Use stand-up Bell pan for the body and two cupcakes put together for the head. Cut a chilled sheet cake 1½″ high into 1½″ strips for legs and arms. Arms are 6″ long, tapered at each end. Legs are 5½″ long, feet 2½″ long. Freeze the cakes.

2. Bake, fill and ice a 9″ × 13″ × 4″ cake for base. Pipe tube 13 message, then stripe sides with tube 22. Pipe reverse shell border at base and top border with tube 17.

3. Assemble the doll in this order. Ice the bell cake and set on base. Set legs against body and ice. Attach feet with toothpicks and ice. All ruffles are done with tube 127. Do ruffle at hem of dress, then bead at top with tube 5, at hem with tube 3. Ice arms and attach with thin dowel rods. Add ruffles on sleeves and bead edges with tube 3. Pipe neck ruffle. Attach head and ice thickly to round. Brush smooth, then add tube 3 beading to neck ruffle. Pipe eyes and buttons with tube 10 and flatten. Do nose with tube 6, mouth with tube 3.

4. Pipe hair with tube 13 and add a perky bow. Pipe candle holders with tube 1F and royal icing and insert candles. Dry. Cake serves about 44.

Birthday cakes for the talkative teens

THREE CHATTY WAYS to greet your favorite teen, who may seem at times to be permanently attached to the telephone. All are fun to make.

Take a message

to the cake top with a telephone shaped of cake and covered with icing stars. Give a real telephone as a gift.

1. Make 15 royal icing daisies in advance, mounting four on 2" long wires. Pipe petals with tube 104. Pipe tube 5 centers, flatten with a damp finger dipped in granulated sugar.

2. Cut telephone handle from a chilled 8" square layer, making it 7" long × 1" × 1" deep. Cut a slant at either end. Make telephone receiver and speaker from two small Wonder Mold cakes. Chill cakes and cut 1" off wide end of each. Ice bottoms smooth. Set aside.

3. Ice a 9" × 13" × 4" sheet cake. Pipe bottom shell border with tube 17. Edge

top with tube 14 shells.

4. Assemble telephone on cake top with icing. Cover all but flat ends with tube 16 stars, building up speaker and receiver rims with more stars. Add tube 2 dots for "holes". Pipe cord and message with tube 2.

5. Trim cake with daisies, positioning stemmed daisies behind handle. Pipe tube 65 leaves. Add Push-in Candle Holders and candles. Serves 24.

Conversation-piece

They'll love a phone like the one grandma used when she was a teen. Shape it of brightly tinted marzipan.

1. Make phone first. (Marzipan recipe, page 23.) Tint ⅔ orange, ⅓ red. Use various sizes of round cutters and Plastic Bell Molds to shape some pieces. Model other pieces by hand. (See diagram at right.)

2. Ice a 9" × 13" × 3" sheet cake and

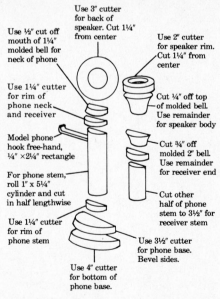

Use 3" cutter for back of speaker. Cut 1¼" from center

Use ½" cut off mouth of 1¼" molded bell for neck of phone

Use 2" cutter for speaker rim. Cut 1¼" from center

Use 1¼" cutter for rim of phone neck and receiver

Cut ¼" off top of molded bell. Use remainder for speaker body

Model phone hook free-hand, ¼" × 2¼" rectangle

Cut ¾" off molded 2" bell. Use remainder for receiver end

For phone stem, roll 1" x 5¼" cylinder and cut in half lengthwise

Cut other half of phone stem to 3½" for receiver stem

Use 1¼" cutter for rim of phone stem

Use 3½" cutter for phone base. Bevel sides.

Use 4" cutter for bottom of phone base.

Cut all but speaker parts in half to lie flat on cake

assemble all of telephone on top except mouthpiece. Pipe tube 6 phone cord. Write tube 2 message, then attach mouthpiece. Pipe tube 2 "holes".

3. Edge cake base and cake top with tube 17 shells. Mark cake sides every 3″ with a toothpick about 1″ above base. Drape two rows of tube 2 string between marks and trim with tube 2 fleur-de-lis. Frame cake with candles in Push-in Candle Holders. Serves 24.

Worth repeating...

your birthday wishes. A brilliant-hued parrot, also a big talker, is your messenger. Impressive but easy!

1. Ice a 9″ × 13″ × 3″ cake and transfer *Celebrate! IV* pattern to cake. Outline with tube 1. Fill in perch with tube 16 stars. Pipe claws with tube 4.

2. Build up breast and wings with icing. Then cover breast with tube 65s feathers, starting at bottom and overlapping

as you move up. Pipe head same as breast, using tube 65s and overlapping as you move upward. Pipe hooked beak with tube 9. Add tube 3 dot for eye.

3. Pipe tail, then wings with tube 104. Overlap as you go, rounding off ends of feathers. Pipe top row of wing feathers in ruffle fashion.

4. Write messages with tube 1. Edge base of cake with tube 19 stars, top with tube 16 shells. Add Push-in Candle Holders and candles. Serves 24.

Sweet sixteen

Time for that first starry-eyed romance. Show her you understand with a charming star-portrait cake.

1. Make soda scene ahead in royal icing. Cover *Celebrate! IV* pattern with wax paper and outline all details with tube 2. Fill in with closely-piped tube 14 stars. Set aside.

2. Ice a 9″ × 13″ × 4″ sheet cake and

position soda scene on cake top. Border bottom of cake with tube 124 ribbon piped in shell fashion. Mark four divisions on 9″ cake sides, six divisions on 13″ back of cake and two divisions on either side of 13″ cake front, leaving a center space for lettering. Pipe tube 103 scallops from mark to mark all around cake sides and write tube 2 message in front.

3. Edge top of cake with tube 103 ribbon piped in shell fashion. Mark sides of cake top into six divisions each and curve tube 103 scallops from mark to mark to frame scene.

4. Trim cake with tube 12 hearts (pipe a pair of shell shapes close together). Add Push-in Candle Holders and candles. Serves 24.

Birthday cheers

Happy way to hail your high school or college hero (or heroine). Lively piped figures add special fun.

1. Make football first. Ice two half-egg Minicakes together and cover with brown icing. Pat with terry cloth towel for pigskin texture. Add tube 55 stripes and laces. Make paper pennants, 3½″ × 2″ and write tube 2 message on each. Attach to iced popsicle sticks.

2. Pipe six cheer leader figures on wax paper. (Icing recipe, page 103.) Begin with tube 2 stick figure outlines, 3½″ tall and 2½″ wide. Make three with arms raised and three with arms outstretched. Turn outlines upside down and pipe tube 2A bodies. Squeeze with heavy pressure, keeping tip of tube buried in icing. Lighten pressure as you move upward to taper top. For arms and legs, insert tip of tube 10 into body and squeeze while moving out. Pipe tube 2A heads and add tube 2 features and tube 1 curly hair. Pipe tube 10 socks and shoes and tube 124 ruffled skirts. Trim jerseys with tube 1 stripes and tube 2 "C" scrolls. Add tube 233 pompons to ends of arms, pulling strings straight up.

3. Ice an oval two-layer cake, and border with tube 10 balls at bottom and tube 7 balls at top. Attach figures to cake sides with icing, alternating raised and outstretched arms. Center football on cake top, back with pennants and frame with candles in Push-in Holders. Serves twelve.

Two words say it all
Shown on page 43

A cake for any birthday child!

1. Make Color Flow plaque. Tape *Celebrate! IV* pattern to flat surface and cover smoothly with wax paper. Outline circle and letters with tube 2 and yellow icing and leaves with tube 1 and light green icing. Flow in thinned icing. Dry thoroughly, at least 48 hours.

2. Bake a 10″ round two-layer cake. Fill, ice and place on foil-covered board. Pipe tube 19 reverse shells around the base of the cake. Pipe tube 18 reverse shells around the top edge. Insert Push-In Candle Holders around side of cake. Starting at center front near bottom border, taper up on either side to near the top border at the center back.

3. Insert candles in holders and drop a tube 13 drape from holder to holder. Attach plaque to cake with dots of icing and sugar cubes. Serves 14.

CIRCUS WAGON *continued*

control, pipe tube 4B bodies and tube 12 heads. Dry, then add tube 104 neck ruffle and tube 102 cuffs. Attach heads to bodies. Pipe feet with tube 6 and hands with tube 4. Cut hats from paper, using pattern, and glue into cone shape. Attach to heads with icing. Pipe tube 13 eyes, then add nose, mouth, pompon, hair and buttons with tube 1. Dry thoroughly.

6. Bake four 9″ x 13″ cake layers. Trim each to 8″ x 11″ and fill to make two 8″ x 11″ two-layer cakes. Assemble as *Celebrate! IV* diagram shows. Cover base with wax paper and ice cake.

7. Pipe tube 14 double shell borders around top and side of cake, and a single shell border at base. Using picture on page 45 as reference, attach trims to cake with mounds of icing. First push in name plaques on each long side, then wheels to conceal styrofoam supports. Add Baroque designs and Angel Musicians. Both long sides are identical.

On front of cake, insert two filigree pedestals for drivers' seats. Add Baroque trims. Attach star to top center on two tube 14 scrolls. Trim back the same, but omit pedestals.

Insert candles in top of cake, then position clowns. Set elephants on board, placing cords in hands of clown drivers. Secure clown to elephant's back. A circus extravaganza that serves 40.

BIRTHDAY JOYS *continued*

cake and add candles. The rockets will each serve two and the base cake will serve 24.

Let's make yarn dolls

1. Make dolls with royal icing. Tape wax paper over *Celebrate! IV* pattern, build up areas for head, body, arms and legs with tube 6. To create yarn effect, use tube 4 and pipe vertical lines on head and body, then lengthwise along arms and legs. When dry, turn over and pipe a "spike" on back with tube 5. Dry, then trim with tube 2.

For sit-up dolls, do not connect legs to body when piping. Dry flat, then turn over and pipe back same as front. Attach legs with icing and prop with cotton balls until dry. Trim with tube 2.

2. Bake a Long Loaf cake and ice with buttercream. Place on foil-covered board. Pipe tube 5 bottom ball border. Push candles into top of cake and set sit-up dolls around them. Attach other dolls to sides of cake by pushing "spikes" into cake. Letter message to your favorite little girl with tube 2. Serves 16.

Quick & Pretty carousel

A breeze to make and a joy to see!

1. Make roll-out cookie dough (recipe on page 147) and tint portions red, yellow and green by kneading in paste food color. Roll dough 1/8″ thick and cut seven large and 18 small daisies with Daisy Cutters. Cut holes in centers of six large daisies with tube 2A and in one with tube 12. Cut centers with tube 2A and place in the tube 2A holes before baking. Leave tube 12 hole empty. Cut holes in centers of small daisies with tube 12. Cut centers with same tube and insert in twelve cookies before baking. Cut two adjacent petals off remaining small daisies before baking. Cut 42 circles of dough with the large end of tube 1. Cut six horses with cutter from Animal set. Place toothpicks on back of legs before baking.

2. Bake a cake in the hexagon ring pan. Also bake a cake in a sliced pineapple can and level top. Ice both smoothly and place hexagon on cake board. Decorate can cake with tube 2B stripes and let icing set.

3. Pipe tube 8 balls on base of hexagon, leaving open spaces at each corner. Place the daisies with two petals removed at the corners, pressing them into the border on either

side. Pipe tube 5 balls around top edge of hexagon. On each side of hexagon, attach one large and two small daisies with icing. Fill center hole with crumpled foil, then attach decorated can cake with icing. Push toothpicks on horses' legs into cake and secure with icing.

4. Attach a 9″ hexagon separator plate in the Circus Tent Top with royal icing. Let icing set a few minutes, then attach the plate to the top of the can cake with icing. Secure round cookies around edge and top of Tent Top with icing. Position large daisy with tube 12 hole on topmost point of Tent Top. Secure candles with dots of icing in the holes in the daisies at the corners of the hexagon and on top of the tent. Hexagon serves twelve and can cake slices into five pieces.

RED RIDING HOOD *continued*

with tube 1, other pieces with tube 3. Trim Red Riding Hood with tube 1. When dry, attach two sticks to the back of each piece with royal icing. Be sure sticks on Riding Hood's legs extend to center of figure.

2. Pipe tube 33 drop flowers with tube 2 centers. Dry. Bake an oval cake, 4″ high. Fill and place on cake board. Ice sides smoothly, then ice top and pat with a clean, damp sponge. Pipe tube 6 ball border around base of cake and tube 5 balls around top. Divide side of cake into twelfths. Drop a string from point to point as guideline, then attach flowers to make a garland. Add a tube 66 leaf at top points of garlands. Pipe birthday message with tube 2.

3. Push sticks on Color Flow pieces into cake. Attach drop flowers to top of cake with dots of icing and add tube 66 leaves. Pipe large tube 21 stars in royal icing and insert a candle in each. Dry. Serves twelve.

Sugar Plum Shop

Rose Garden. Decorating
directions on page 74

Celebrate!
MAY/JUNE...the months of love and romance

Cakes for love's most important celebrations

THE WEDDING CAKE is the symbol of love and the centerpiece of love's celebration. No wedding, however small and intimate, can be celebrated without its cake.

So lavish all your artistry and skill in the decoration of the wedding cake. Use love's traditional signs—hearts, flowers, cupids, lace and ribbon bows in its adornment. This cake will always be remembered as an expression of love's promise.

Rose Bouquet

Here's a new idea for the wedding celebration—a petite heart-shaped cake for the parents of the bride and one for the parents of the groom are set beside the wedding cake.

DECORATE THE WEDDING CAKE. This most feminine of pale pink cakes is lavished with bouquets and sprays of pastel flowers. Piped baby's breath makes the flower arrangements especially airy and dainty.

1. Make royal icing flowers in advance. The baby's breath is quick and easy to achieve. Twist ten or twelve lengths of fine florists' wire into a sprig. Pull out many tube 1 points on the end of each wire. Push sprig into styrofoam to dry. Make tube 101s forget-me-nots and roses with tubes 103 and 104. Mount on wires. Pipe leaves directly on wires with tube 66.

Arrange flowers into one large bouquet, two medium and three small clusters and one medium spray.

2. Bake, fill and ice two-layer tiers—14″ square, 10″ round and 6″

Continued on page 74

Rose Bouquet
Decorating directions at left

Rose Garden
for a
summer wedding
shown on page 71

Rose Bouquet
for a
new tradition
continued from
page 72

Rose Glow
for a
sophisticated bride
shown on
opposite page

THE MOST BEAUTIFUL SETTING for a summer wedding is a garden. This stately cake is just as lovely as a garden flower. The sides of the tiers are decorated with a lavish and intricate-looking design. Fresh roses are set between the tiers.

1. Make about four dozen drop flowers using tubes 33 and 225. Bake, fill and ice 6" round, 10" round and 14" square two-layer tiers. Assemble cake on ruffle-edged board with Corinthian pillars and 6" and 10" round separator plates. Insert clipped-off dowel rods into the two bottom tiers to support tiers above.

2. Using 3¼" and 2" heart-shaped cookie cutters as pattern presses, press design on sides of all three tiers. Then pipe top and bottom shell borders on all tiers. Use tube 22 on bottom of 14" tier and tube 17 on top. Pipe shells with tube 17 on bottom of 10" tier and tube 16 on top. The 6" tier has tube 16 shells on the bottom and tube 15 on top. Edge around separator plates with tube 17 scallops.

3. Now tint icing pink and make side designs using tube 16 to make swirls, reverse shells and fleurs-de-lis. Attach drop flowers with dots of icing and pipe leaves with a parchment cone cut in a "V" shape.

4. Add the finishing touches. Arrange a bouquet of fresh roses. Set plastic Heart Base upside down, line with clear plastic wrap and fill with Oasis. Dampen the Oasis and arrange the bouquet of roses. Attach some drop flowers to Card-Holder cherub with icing and place between upper pillars. Attach a sprinkling of drop flowers to Rhapsody of Love ornament and place on top of cake. Place the prepared bouquet of fresh roses between the lower pillars. See how easy it is to create a beautiful wedding cake in a short time! Serves 150.

round. Assemble on a ruffle-edged, foil-covered board. Insert dowel rods, clipped off level with cake top, into 14" tier to support 10" tier. Elevate 6" tier with 6" round separator plates and Crystal Clear pillars.

3. On 14" tier, pipe tube 16 shell borders, leaving an open space in the top border in front. Then, using tube 17, make curves over bottom shell border. Make more curves in a semicircle on the front of the tier, beginning at the end of the top shells. Add tube 13 stars on sides of tier. Attach Angelino with icing.

4. On 10" tier, make tube 16 shells and curves at base. Trace four semicircular areas spaced evenly around sides of the tier. Fill top border areas between semicircles with tube 15 shells. Add tube 17 curves to semicircles, then add stars with tube 13 to sides of tier.

5. Do top tier similar to others. Pipe tube 15 shells and curves at base, tube 15 shells at top. Stars on sides are tube 13.

6. Tie ribbon around large bouquet and small spray, leaving long ends. Place large bouquet on top of 6" tier. Place Petite Bridal Couple between pillars and two medium clusters on either side. Set two Card-Holder cherubs on bottom tier. Place ends of ribbon in hands of one and small spray in hands of other. Arrange a small and medium cluster beside each cherub and another small cluster beneath Angelino. Serves 150.

DECORATE THE PARENTS' CAKES

Each of these Mini-Tier cakes is decorated in a very similar manner as the top tier of the wedding cake. The same flowers are used, but the roses are piped with smaller tubes. Trim the middle tier with kneeling Cherub. Each of these cakes serves twelve.

THIS MOST UNUSUAL and handsome cake will delight a bride who appreciates good design. Trim is a beautiful cascade of glowing roses. The flowers lift off for easy serving.

1. Pipe the roses first. Fit three decorating bags with tube 104. Fill one with yellow for the center, one with paler yellow for the first row of petals and one with white for the rest. Pipe the roses and mount all on wire stems. Pipe tube 67 leaves on wires. Tape into clusters.

2. Bake two-layer tiers—14" square, 12" and 9" heart. Fill and ice with buttercream. Assemble on a foil-covered board, inserting clipped-off dowel rods into the lower two tiers to support the upper tiers.

3. On bottom tier, create base border by piping tube 17 garlands and framing them with tube 5 bulbs. Pipe tube 6 bulbs for top border. Divide sides of tier into fourths. Drop a tube 3 string from point to point, then drop more strings below to increase from two strings to five as you move back from the corner. Trim string intersections with a curl of icing.

On the 12" tier, pipe base and top borders the same as bottom tier. Divide side of tier into sixths. Drop a tube 3 string from point to point, then drop more strings below these so that at the point of the heart there are four strings that decrease to one as you move to the back. Trim intersections with a curl of icing.

Pipe top and base borders of the 9" tier with tube 5 bulbs. Divide the side into fourths, then drop a tube 3 string from point to point. Drop more strings below these so there are three strings at the point of the heart, decreasing back to one. Trim intersections with a curl of icing.

4. Secure ornament to top of cake. Arrange clusters of roses on tiers to create a cascade. Serves 170.

Rose Glow
Decorating
directions at left

75

THE GROOM'S CAKE, a British tradition, has become a popular practice in many American weddings also. While the wedding cake is cut and eaten at the reception, the groom's cake is cut and the pieces distributed as a keepsake or for single girls to "dream on." It can also be served on a sweet table. It is a lovely tradition to add to the wedding.

Chocolate Scroll *upper left*

This elegant cake was designed to complement Baroque, page 85.

Bake a 10″ × 4″ round, two-layer cake. Ice in light chocolate buttercream and place on a serving tray or foil-covered cake board. Using *Celebrate! IV* pattern, mark scroll design on top and side. Pipe scrolls with tube 16 and dark chocolate buttercream or Chocolate Canache (see recipe below). Add a tube 16 star border around base of cake. Cuts into 48 pieces, 1″ × 2″.

Fruit cake ring *upper right*

Bake a fruitcake in a ring pan following the Best-ever Applesauce Fruitcake recipe, submitted by one of our readers, on page 29, or use your own favorite. Place the cooled cake on a serving tray. Brush cake with apricot glaze (heat one cup apricot preserves to boiling and strain). Then arrange a bouquet of fresh flowers in the Heart Bowl or other vase and place it in the center hole of the cake. This simple, handsome cake slices into about 40 keepsake-size pieces.

Chocolate Rose *lower left*

Topped with a marzipan plaque and roses piped with Chocolate Canache, this cake has a Continental flair.

CHOCOLATE CANACHE

This delicious mixture pipes beautiful roses and borders. The flavor is outstanding.

    1 cup German sweet chocolate, cut up
    ⅓ cup whipping cream
    1½ tablespoons confectioners' sugar

Temper chocolate (see page 44), then reheat to 86° - 88°F. Mix cream and sugar together, then stir into chocolate until thoroughly mixed. Mixture will be very soft and "soupy." Place in refrigerator for about ten minutes. If it sets too hard, allow it come to room temperature and stir well before filling cone and piping roses. Canache may be kept in the refrigerator for weeks if well-covered. When ready to use, bring to

Add romantic tradition

to the wedding

with a handsome

groom's cake

room temperature and stir.

1. Pipe roses with tube 104 and Chocolate Canache. You will need nine roses and two buds. Refrigerate until ready to use. Pipe tube 67 leaves on wax paper with same mixture, but substitute 1 cup of tempered unsweetened dark chocolate for the German sweet chocolate. Reheat to 90° - 92°F, then proceed.

2. Roll out a piece of marzipan (recipe, page 23) about ⅛″ thick. Cut a 3″ × 4″ oval from it using *Celebrate! IV* pattern or your own. Dry. Pipe the names with tube 2.

3. Bake a 9″ × 13″ × 4″ cake. Ice top smoothly and sides heavily. Place on a foil-covered board. Using an icing comb, make a wavy design on the sides of the cake. Pipe tube 17 rosettes around the base and tube 14 shells around the top. Secure marzipan plaque to cake top and circle it with tube 14 shells. Pipe tube 7 stems with dark Chocolate Canache and add tube 2 thorns. Secure roses and leaves in position with dots of icing. Cake cuts into about 48 pieces.

Chocolate Hexagon *lower right*

This is another cake with a Continental look. Covered with glossy Chocolate Fondant and trimmed with marzipan and a stand-up piped ornament, it's a masterpiece.

CHOCOLATE FONDANT

    6 cups confectioners' sugar
    7 ounces water
    2 tablespoons corn syrup
    4 ounces unsweetened, melted chocolate
    1 teaspoon almond flavoring

Combine water and corn syrup. Add to sugar in a saucepan and stir over low heat until well mixed and heated until just warm, 100°F. Stir in melted chocolate and almond flavoring. Place iced cake on cooling rack with a pan or cookie sheet beneath it. Pour fondant over cake, flowing from center and moving out in a circular motion. Yields four cups—enough to cover an 8″ cake.

1. Bake a 12″ × 4″ hexagon cake and ice with a thin coat of buttercream. Make a double recipe of Chocolate Fondant and pour over cake. Let harden, then transfer cake to a foil-covered board.

2. Roll out marzipan ⅛″ thick (recipe page 23). Cut a 4½″ circle and 18 small 1″ hearts. Also cut 18 circles, 2″ in diameter. Trim off one-fourth of the circle and cut out a 1″ heart from the remaining piece. Dry all flat.

3. Using *Celebrate! IV* pattern, make six scroll pieces for top ornament. Pipe with tube 14 and royal icing. Dry, then turn over and pipe again. When dry, assemble with royal icing on 4½″ circle.

4. Place ornament in center of cake and secure with icing. Secure hearts around it. Add circles with hearts removed around base of cake. This fabulous cake cuts into about 50 pieces, 1″ × 2″.

Celebration
Decorating directions, page 80

Rose Crochet
Decorating directions, page 80

ADORNED WITH CHERUBS and garlands of drop flowers, this elegant cake appears very grand, but is really quite easy to decorate.

*Celebration
for a lavish
reception*
shown on page 78

THIS BEAUTIFULLY UNIQUE wedding cake is adorned with bouquets of wild roses. "Crocheted-look" lace in a rose pattern gives an airy effect.

*Rose Crochet
a uniquely beautiful
bridal cake*
shown on page 79

ORANGE BLOSSOMS, the traditional bridal flowers, wreath the tiers of this lovely cake. Simple but lavish side trims add interest and design.

*Orange Blossom
for the bride
who loves tradition*
shown on
opposite page

1. Make many pink and white drop flowers with tubes 33 and 225. Dry.

2. Bake 14″ x 5″ three-layer square, 10″ x 4″ two-layer square and 8″ x 3″ round tiers. Ice and assemble on a foil-covered board with 7″ Corinthian pillars and 12″ square separator plates. Edge lower separator plate with tube 6. Pipe triple bead border around base of 14″ tier and single bead border around top with tube 8. Attach Twin Angels to each side of tier with icing, secure drop flowers and pipe tube 104 bows. Add tube 66 leaves. Attach a Cherub Concerto figure between front pillars and secure drop flowers at his feet.

3. Pipe triple bead border around base of 10″ tier, single bead border around top with tube 6. On each side, pipe a garland with tube 8, attach drop flowers and add tube 66 leaves. Secure Angelinos at ends of garlands with icing.

4. Pipe single tube 6 bead borders around top and bottom of 8″ tier. Divide side into fourths and pipe a mound of icing at each division. Attach drop flowers and pipe tube 66 leaves, then pipe tube 2 stems and a tube 103 bow. Insert three Flower Spikes into top of cake. Secure a Cherub Concerto figure in front of spikes and attach a sprinkling of drop flowers.

5. Turn Heart Base upside down, line with plastic wrap and fill with Oasis. Dampen Oasis and insert fresh flowers. Set between pillars. Insert more fresh flowers into Flower Spikes on cake top. Serves 178.

1. Using *Celebrate! IV* patterns, tape large and small wing patterns to flat surface and lace piece patterns to 16″ curved surface. You will need eight of each. Pipe with tube 1 and royal icing. When wings dry, turn over and over-pipe main lines.

2. Pipe six dozen tube 103 wild roses and four dozen rosebuds. Mount all on wires. Pipe tube 67 leaves on wires. Tape all into sprays.

3. Bake a tier using the Party Ring Mold and two 16″ round layers. Fill layers and ice tiers smoothly with boiled icing. Assemble on foil-covered cake board using 5″ Corinthian pillars and 12″ round separator plates. Insert clipped-off dowel rods into 16″ tier to support ring tier. Pipe tube 7 scallops around base separator plate and tube 7 bottom bulb borders on both tiers.

4. Ice two styrofoam half-balls and attach in Heart Bowl and to upside down plate of small Heart Base with icing. Insert flower sprays into ball halves. Secure flower-filled bowl in center of ring tier and arrangement in plate between pillars with icing.

5. Divide tiers into eighths, making sure markings line up on both tiers. Attach small wings to top tier, large wings to bottom tier and curved lace pieces between large wings with dots of icing. Serves 160.

1. Make many orange blossoms on foil-covered slighted indented flower nail. Pipe five tube 81 pointed petals. Pipe two upright petals to form cup in center. Dry, then top cup with tube 1 dots. Mount on wires. For buds, pipe a tube 5 ball on florists' wire. Add tube 1 sepals. Pipe tube 67 leaves on wires. Tape all into clusters.

2. Bake 6″ x 3″, 10″ x 4″ round and 14″ x 4″ square tiers. Fill, ice and assemble on ruffle-edged cake board, using 5″ Corinthian pillars and two 6″ round separator plates.

3. Divide sides of 14″ tier into sixths. At each division, pipe a tube 19 column and tube 16 fleur-de-lis. Complete base border with tube 16 stars. Drop tube 3 strings between columns. Add tube 16 stars above strings and at base of fleur-de-lis.

4. Pipe tube 18 bottom shell border around 10″ tier. Divide side of tier into twelfths. Pipe freehand hearts with tube 16 around side and add stars between and beneath them. Edge lower separator plate with tube 16 scallops. Arrange flowers around base of tier for wreath.

5. Divide 6″ tier into eighths. At each division pipe a tube 16 fleur-de-lis. Pipe tube 16 base star border. Pipe tube 13 stars above fleurs-de-lis. Add tube 16 top shell border.

6. Glue bridal couple to Heart Base and secure to cake top. Attach orange blossoms to base with icing for wreath. Ice a half-ball of styrofoam and insert flower clusters. Attach between pillars, extending more clusters out. Serves 162.

Orange Blossom
Decorating directions at left.

81

Daisy Bower
Decorating
directions, page 84

Daisy Chain *shown on page 82*

1. Make about 125 white daisies with royal icing and tubes 102 and 103. Pipe tube 5 centers and flatten with finger dipped in granulated sugar. Dry within curved surface. Pipe leaves on wire with tube 67. Pipe tube 5 spikes on back of about 65 daisies and set aside. Mount remaining daisies on wire and arrange into one large and seven small clusters.

2. Bake, fill and ice two-layer tiers—6″ hexagon, 10″ round and 15″ hexagon. Assemble on ruffle-edged cake board, inserting dowel rods clipped off level with top into 15″ and 10″ tiers. Use 5″ Corinthian Pillars between 6″ hexagon separator plates to elevate top tier.

3. Pipe bottom bulb border with tube 7. Drop a string guideline from point to point on lower hexagon tier to form an arc on side of each panel. Fill top of tier and area within arc with tube 2 cornelli lace. Edge panels and cornelli area with tube 3 beading.

4. Pipe tube 7 bulb border around base of 10″ tier and tube 5 bulb border around top. Divide side of cake into sixths, then each section into thirds. Lower dots defining middle third to about 1″ above border. Using tube 2, drop double strings between divisions, adding a swirl at each intersection.

Pipe a mound of icing on separator plate and attach large cluster of daisies. Make six garlands on side of tier by pushing in spiked daisies on mounds of icing. Add tube 67 leaves. Add a ribbon bow and daisy to top of tier at points of garlands. Edge separator plate with tube 16.

5. On top tier, drop a string guideline on each panel. Fill lower area with tube 2 cornelli lace. Pipe bottom bulb border with tube 5, and edge curves with tube 2.

6. Tie ribbon bows to six small clusters. Set on cake board, centering one in each panel. Attach Winged Cherubs to sides of top tier with icing. Place Love's Doves ornament on top of cake. Insert Flower Spike behind it and arrange small daisy cluster in it. Daisy Chain serves 120.

Daisy Bower *shown on page 83*

A masterpiece cake. Dainty gum paste baskets are filled with daisies and more daisies flower on the arch that crowns the top tier.

1. Make gum paste baskets. Using recipe and technique on page 22, roll out gum paste, then mold over Australian basket nail, dusted with cornstarch. Trim to fit. Dry 24 hours, then remove from nail. Pipe tube 13 basketweave over basket, adding tube 13 rope border around top and shells around bottom. Make handle by rolling a long gum paste cylinder and bending into an arch the width of basket top and about 3″ high. Secure a small piece of styrofoam in each basket with royal icing. Attach dried handle with icing.

2. Use this quick method to make many Philippine-style daisies. Pipe centers on 5″ pieces of florists' wire. Bend one end into a tiny hook, insert into tube 7 and squeeze bag while pulling out. Do many of these centers at once, then dry. Holding wire with center up, start pulling out short tube 1 lines halfway down center. Pipe two or three rows close together. Hang upside down to dry. Then holding wire upside down, pipe tube 81 petals around center. Hang upside down until dry. Pipe tube 67 leaves on wires. Insert clusters of flowers and leaves into baskets.

3. Assemble ornament for top of cake. Remove gates and fence from Picket Archway. Twine wires of flowers and leaves on arch, then glue Angel Fountain on base.

4. Bake 6″×3″, 9″×4″ and 15″×4″ petal tiers. Fill and ice. Assemble. Glue four legs to bottom of 16″ plate from Tall Tier Stand. Use 16″ plate to support 15″ tier and 10″ plate to support upper tiers.

5. Pipe tube 14 shells around center post on top of 15″ tier. Pipe tube 16 bottom shell border. On side of each petal of bottom tier, pipe a tube 14 fleur-de-lis topped with star. Frame with tube 14 curves and scrolls. Pipe tube 14 top shell border.

6. On 9″ tier, pipe tube 15 bottom shell border. Drop tube 13 strings on each petal. Pipe tube 13 stars below. Add tube 13 top shell border.

7. Pipe tube 14 bottom shell border on 6″ tier. Center a tube 13 fleur-de-lis topped with star on each petal. Add two "C" shapes beneath it and a star above it with tube 13. Top border is tube 13 shells.

8. Attach ornament to top of cake and trim with flowers and leaves. Secure baskets to top of 15″ tier. Attach daisies and leaves at base. This stunning cake serves 90 guests.

Baroque, *opposite page*

This magnificent cake is adorned with tiny gum paste flowers in garlands and baskets. Piped scrolls complete the design.

MAKE BASKETS

1. Use Australian Basket nail as form. Roll out gum paste (recipe page 22) and cut a strip 6½″ × 1⅝″. Make grooves ⅛″ apart with thin cardboard. Dust nail with cornstarch and set in styrofoam block. Carefully smooth strip around nail, joining ends with egg white. Dry overnight and remove from nail.

2. Roll out gum paste ⅛″ thick and set basket on it to make impression for base. Set basket aside, cut out base. Brush edge with egg white and set basket on base to attach. Dry. Cut three ⅛″ strips about 6½″ long, brush with egg white and wrap

continued on page 90

Cakes for love's most important celebrations

CREATE REGAL CAKES to make Father's Day and Mother's Day extra special. The ornaments on top of the cakes are fashioned of gum paste. If you plan ahead and make the ornaments well in advance, the cakes are much quicker to decorate. So decorate these impressive cakes to honor the best-loved couple in your life on the special days set aside just for them.

Plan a royal Celebration

Dad...he's King of Hearts

Dad will truly feel like a king when he sees this distinctive cake made just for him.

1. Make gum paste following the recipe and instructions on page 22. Roll out the gum paste 1/16″ thick. Using *Celebrate! IV* patterns, cut crown, shield, shield scroll, heart and side scroll. Roll edges on scrolls and dry all the pieces on a flat surface. Pipe tube 2 beading on shield, tube 1 trim on crown and heart. Add message on side scroll with tube 1. Assemble plaque for top of cake with mounds of royal icing and dry thoroughly.

2. Bake a 9″ × 13″ × 4″ cake and ice smoothly with buttercream. Place on a foil-covered cake board. Pipe tube 18 bottom shell border. Make your own patterns for the scroll designs on the side and top of the cake, or mark them freehand. Mark the scroll design on the sides of the cake with a toothpick, then pipe with tube 18. Mark scroll design on top of cake, making sure to leave center uncovered for plaque to be attached. Use shield scroll pattern to help you to determine the size of the area to be left uncovered. Pipe scrolls on the cake top with tube 18, then over-pipe with tube 17. Trim top edge of the cake with a tube 16 shell border.

3. Attach gum paste side scroll and heart with icing. Then attach the plaque to the top of the cake with sugar cubes and royal icing and it will be easy to lift off for cutting the cake. Bring Dad in for a royal surprise! Serves 24.

Mother...Queen of Hearts

Mother will really appreciate the extra care taken to make her lovely cake so very special.

MAKE GUM PASTE CROWN

1. Make a recipe of gum paste following the instructions on page 22. Draw a 4″ diameter circle on a piece of paper, tape to a flat surface and cover with wax paper. Roll out gum paste 1/16″ thick, and, using *Celebrate! IV* patterns, cut strip for base of crown. Form into a circle, attaching ends with egg white, and place it on edge on the circle drawn on paper. Dry. Divide into sixths, cut small tabs from pattern and attach at each division with egg white.

2. Make a 2″ diameter cardboard cylinder and cover with wax paper. Secure to table near edge with tape. Cut strips for top of crown and dry on cylinder, letting end to be attached to center of crown hang down over edge of table. Cut center circle and heart and dry all pieces 24 hours.

3. Assemble crown with royal icing. (See diagram.) Place a 1¾″ high block of styrofoam in center of crown base and place center circle on top of it. Then attach top strips of crown, matching ends with tabs on base and edge of center circle. Dry.

4. Attach a piece of florists' wire to back of heart with royal icing. Dry, then pipe tube 1s name and beading. Over-pipe beading with clear piping gel for a "jeweled" look.

5. Figure pipe twelve tiny hearts on wax paper with tube 2. Dry. Attach to crown with royal icing and brush hearts with clear piping gel. Add dots of gold piping gel on base and top strips of crown. Pipe a tube 14 rosette with stiffened royal icing on center circle. Insert wire on heart into rosette and prop in position until dry. Lift crown carefully and remove styrofoam block.

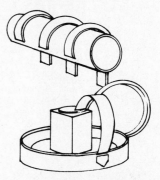

DECORATE THE CAKE

1. With royal icing and tube 104, pipe about 16 daisies. Add tube 7 centers and flatten with a finger dipped in granulated sugar. Also pipe many forget-me-nots with tube 101s. Center with a tube 1 dot. Figure pipe eight hearts with tube 5 and 16 smaller hearts with tube 3. Dry flowers and hearts thoroughly.

2. Bake a 12″ x 4″ petal cake and ice smoothly. Set on serving tray or foil-covered cake board.

3. Pipe tube 5 beading around base of cake. Add a tube 7 zigzag garland on each petal of cake, covering bottom border in center of petal. Edge with tube 3 beading. Drop a series of four tube 3 strings on each petal, beginning a little higher than halfway up side of cake. Attach the smaller figure piped hearts to ends of strings with dots of icing.

4. For top border, pipe a tube 7 zigzag on top of cake and pipe tube 3 beading on either side of it. Attach larger figure piped hearts with dots of icing at inside points of top border. Dry, then brush hearts with clear piping gel for a sparkling effect.

5. Attach forget-me-nots and daisies to sides and at base of cake with dots of icing. Pipe tube 66 leaves. Place crown carefully on top of cake. Present Mother with her cake, fit for a queen! Serves 26.

Happy cakes
for Mom and Dad

It's the time for children of all ages to show their love for their sterling parents. Here, four charming ways.

Breakfast in bed

Dad gets the royal treatment on his day. Even young children can help model the marzipan figures, cheerful quilt and tray of breakfast. Under all: real cake.

1. The 3 figures. All the marzipan figures are modeled the same way. (Recipe, page 23.) Legs start with cylinders, bodies are bell shapes, arms are cylinders with mitten-shaped hands added. Heads are balls. Feet are out-size so figures can stand alone. (Here, father figure is under cover, so a roughly triangular shape will serve for legs.) Parts are joined with egg white with half-toothpicks inserted to secure heads to bodies. Pipe hair, features and buttons with tube 2, collars with tube 101, package trim with tube 1. Make father's body 2" high, arms 2½" long, head ⅞" diameter, leg piece 3½" long. See page 66 for construction of children, proportionately smaller. (Boy should be about 4½" tall, girl about 4" tall.)

2. Breakfast tray. Cut a 2¼" × 1¾" piece of marzipan, add little cylinders for handles. Model tiny plates, juice glass, eggs, toast, cup by hand.

3. The bed. Make gingerbread headboard. (Recipe, page 147.) Cut out using *Celebrate! IV* pattern, bake, cool and outline with tube 2 and Color Flow icing. Flow in with thinned icing. For bed, cut a 9" square cake in half and stack for 9" × 4½" × 3" size. Ice bed smoothly. Edge bed with tube 127D dust ruffle, topped with tube 4 beading. Ice headboard to bed. Model a 2¼" × 1½" pillow from untinted marzipan.

4. To assemble. Prop father comfortably in bed. Add quilt. Cut ⅛" rolled marzipan to 8" × 11". Score lightly with ruler into 1" diamond pattern. Lay over bed. Fold back top, paint with food color thinned with kirsch. Trim with tube 4 beading and tube 1 scallops. Set tray on bed, children around it. Serves about six.

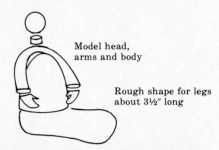

Model head, arms and body

Rough shape for legs about 3½" long

Pipe a portrait

Dad's smiling face tops an easy-to-decorate cake. And the portrait is his to save as a memento.

1. Make portrait first. Cover *Celebrate! IV* pattern with waxed paper and outline all details with tube 2. Fill in with tube 13 stars, add tube 4 eyes, tube 11 cheeks, tube 2 mouth.

2. Bake, fill and ice a 10″ × 4″ two-layer cake. Mark pattern on cake top except for face. Ice center of cake blue.

3. Position face on blue circle. Border with tube 133 rope frame and scroll. Pipe tube 3 letters. At base of cake, alternate tube 22 upright shells and tube 3 dots; edge with tube 22 horizontal shells. Border top of cake with tube 20 shells. Serves 14.

Say something sweet

Shape luscious marzipan letters and put them all together to spell Mother. Pretty, easy and sure to please her.

1. Make marzipan (recipe, page 23.) Divide, tint and roll out ¼″ thick. Cut letters with Alphabet Cookie Cutters and flowers with violet cutter from Flower Garden Set. Cut large 3″ heart and small 1″ hearts with Heart Biscuit Cutters.

2. Bake, fill and ice an 8″ two-layer square cake. Border with tube 16 shells and invert small hearts on bottom border. Use picture as guide to position letters, heart and flowers on cake top. Serves twelve.

Put your heart in it

Sweet, simple cake blushes with hearts, ribbons and flowers. Pretty tribute for Mother. Easy fun for you.

1. Make tube 225 drop flowers. Bake, fill and ice a 10″ × 4″ two-layer round cake. Add tube 8 bottom bulb border, tube 6 top bulb border.

2. Mark heart shapes with 4″ Heart Cutter on cake top and 2″ cutter on cake sides. Outline heart on top with tube 2. Edge all hearts with tube 3 beading. Flow Quick Fondant (recipe, page 13) in large top heart. Frame with tube 104 ruffle and add tube 2 message. Write "Mother" with tube 1 in alternate small hearts on side.

3. Make a mark between points of small hearts and pipe tube 104 ribbon garlands. Trim garlands, empty hearts and cake top with flowers and tube 65 leaves. Serves 14.

Give the graduate
a bunch of good luck

Plan a family party for the graduate with this cake as the centerpiece. The horseshoe shape and the shamrocks say "lots of good luck" and the shamrock flowers add pretty color.

1. Bake a cake in the horseshoe pan. You'll need just one cake mix. Ice smoothly and set on cake board. Pipe a tube 17 shell border at base.

2. Divide outer curving side of horseshoe into twelfths and mark on top edge of cake. Drop a double tube 3 string from mark to mark and at ends of cake. Make tassels by piping a little rope from points of string with tube 1. Pipe tube 1 fringe, top with a tube 4 ball and add tube 1 binding. Pipe top shell border with tube 15. Add tube 2 script message.

3. Use royal icing to pipe the sham-

rocks. Line a 1¼" two-piece lily nail with foil. With tube 101, pipe five petals. Starting in center of nail, move tube over outer edge of nail, then back to center. Add tube 1 dot in center. Jiggle your hand for ruffled effect. When flowers are dry, mount on wire stems.

Pipe leaves directly on wire on wax paper with tube 103. Pipe center heart-shaped lobe first, then pipe a heart shape on either side of it. Dry thoroughly. Tape stems of flowers and leaves together into a bouquet and set on cake. Serves twelve.

Baroque *continued*

around basket. Add a ring made by cutting a circle with tube 1A and removing center with tube 2A. When basket is thoroughly dry, insert a small piece of styrofoam, securing with royal icing, and arrange bouquet of wired blossoms.

3. Make four half-baskets the same way, but cover only half of nail.

MAKE GUM PASTE FLOWERS

Tint equal amounts of gum paste in three pastel shades. Using forget-me-not and violet cutters, cut many flowers from each color. Press each petal from tip to center with model-

ing stick 5, then dry. Pipe tube 1 in centers. Mount larger flowers on wire stems to place in whole basket.

DECORATE CAKE

1. Bake, fill and ice 14", 10" and 6" square, two-layer tiers. Assemble on a foil-covered board using an 11" square separator plate, a 12" round separator plate and 5" Grecian Pillars. Insert clipped off dowel rods into lower and middle tiers. Transfer *Celebrate! IV* patterns to tiers.

Pipe shell borders—tube 18 for base tier, tube 16 for center tier and tube 14 for top tier. Edge separator plate

with tube 13.

2. Pipe all scrolls and trim on tiers with tube 16, then over-pipe with tube 14. Drop string guidelines to mark position of garlands on base and top tiers. Pipe ends of garlands with tube 13, then pipe a heavy curve with tube 12. Press in flowers.

3. Attach half-baskets to sides of 10" tier on mounds of icing. Pipe a large mound of icing above each basket and press in flowers. Trim Celestial Twins ornament with flowers and set on cake. Place basket within pillars. Baroque serves 160.

Celebrate!

JULY/AUGUST...time for fun and sunny cakes

A salute to Hawaii!
Decorating directions, page 92

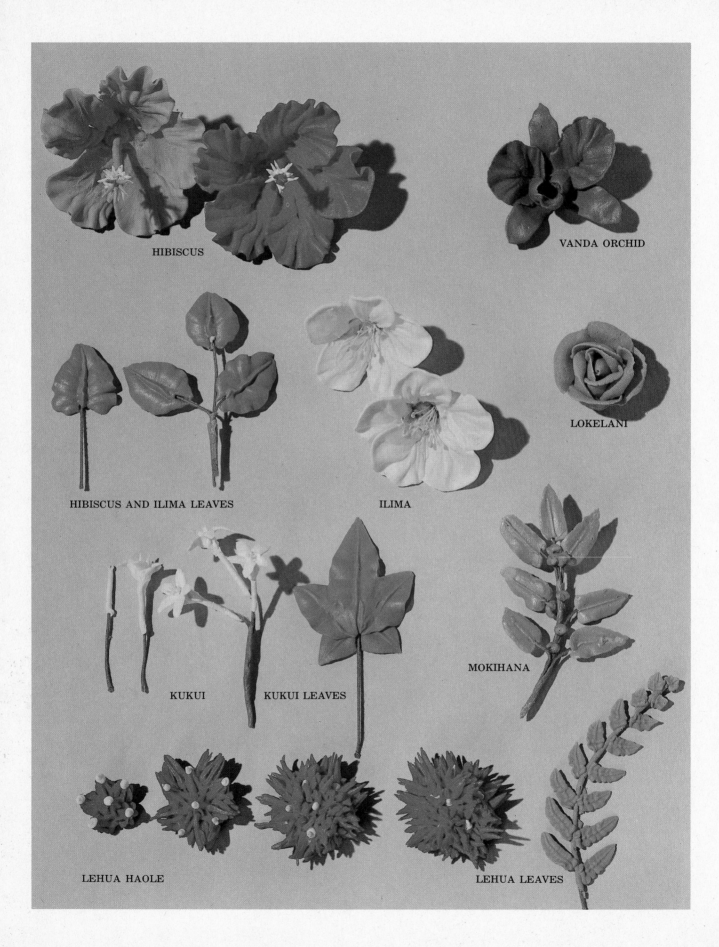

HIBISCUS

VANDA ORCHID

HIBISCUS AND ILIMA LEAVES

ILIMA

LOKELANI

KUKUI

KUKUI LEAVES

MOKIHANA

LEHUA HAOLE

LEHUA LEAVES

A Salute to Hawaii's Bicentennial

On the morning of January 18, 1778, Captain James Cook of England's royal navy with his two ships, HMS *Resoluton* and HMS *Discovery* sighted the island of Oahu. Now, 200 years later, the islands of Hawaii celebrate the bicentennial of their discovery by the Western world. Since that time Hawaii has been a monarchy, a United States territory, and finally, on August 21, 1959, our fiftieth state.

Anyone who has ever been to these smiling islands has fallen in love with them. In Hawaii, flowers bloom all year, the season's always summer, the breezes are gentle and the greeting is *Aloha*. "Welcome, I am glad you are here. You are my friend, I love you. Goodbye, return quickly." Aloha!

The Bicentennial cake
This splendid cake reflects the beauty and color of the sunny Hawaiian islands. Five cakes baked in the blossom pans represent the five principal islands, Oahu, Kauai, Molokai, Hawaii and Maui, with their corrugated, lava-formed mountains. Each is adorned with its island flower. The brilliant hibiscus, state flower of Hawaii, cascades down one side. Stylized shapes of the feathered helmets worn by Hawaiian chiefs form a side border on the base tier. A little replica of the great double canoes in which the first Hawaiians sailed from the South Seas to the islands is placed to the side of the cake and the flag of Hawaii flies over all.

1. Make the trims in advance. Pipe the flowers in royal icing as described below. Make the Color Flow letters by taping patterns to stiff board and taping wax paper over. Outline with tube 1 and fill in thickly with thinned icing to create rounded effect. Tape the helmet patterns to stiff board and tape wax paper over. Using royal icing, outline with tube 1 and fill in with tube 13 stars. You will need about 15 helmets facing right and 15 facing left. Page 106 tells how to make the canoe.

2. Prepare the tiers. The base tier is a two-layer 12" x 18" sheet cake. Bake two layers in 10" round pans and one layer in a 10" square pan to form the oval upper tier. Fill the round layers and cut in half to form semi-circles. Cut the 10" square layer in half and fill and stack to form a 5" x 10" two-layer rectangle. Cut a 10" x 15" oval cake board. Center rectangle on board, place semi-circles on either side. Bake 5 cakes in blossom pans.

3. Ice and assemble the cake. Set the base tier on a 12" x 18" cake board. Ice the sides in yellow and the top blue. Ice the oval tier in blue and set on the base tier, ½" from the back and 1" from the left side. Ice the blossom cakes and arrange on oval tier.

4. Decorate the cake. Tape real lemon leaves to edge of a 14" x 20" cake board and position cake in center. Stir blue food color into boiled icing, but do not tint evenly. Let some white streaks remain. Swirl over top of base tier and all over oval tier for a watery "ocean" look. Pipe tube 18 base shell border and tube 16 top border. Attach helmets and Color Flow letters with dots of icing. Arrange flowers on cake and set canoe on the "ocean". Insert flag. "Hawaii" serves 78.

The flowers of the islands
HIBISCUS, the state flower of Hawaii. This large beautiful flower grows on shrubs all over the islands in a multitude of colors. The scarlet variety is the state's floral emblem.

Line a 2¼" two-piece lily nail with foil. Pipe five ruffled petals. Using tube 104, start at base of petal with light pressure. Increase pressure and jiggle your hand as you move out to edge of petal, then return to base as you decrease pressure. Dry. Pipe a little mound of icing in center of flower and insert a 1¾" curved florists' wire. Fit a decorating cone with tube 4 and push over wire. Pull out to cover wire. Pipe tube 1 stamens at tip, surround with tube 1 yellow stamens. The shaded effect in the orange flower is achieved by brushing with thinned icing.

Pipe leaves directly on florists' wire with tube 70. Tape together in groups of three.

VANDA ORCHID. This little baby orchid is often made into flowery leis.

Line a 1⅝" two-piece lily nail with foil, but do not press the foil all the way to the base of the nail.

Pipe three slender leaf shapes with tube 326. Pipe a ruffled, rounded petal on either side of the top "leaf" with tube 103. Use tube 79 to pipe upstanding center throat. Pull out a cup shape at the base of each ruffled petal, then join with a third cup shape pulled out a little longer.

ILIMA, the flower of Oahu. Leis made from this wild flower were once worn only by chiefs, and called royal leis.

Pipe the petals just as for the hibiscus, but use a 1⅝" two-piece lily nail and tube 103. After drying, pipe a mound in the center of the flower and insert artificial stamens. Pipe leaves same as hibiscus leaves.

LOKELANI, the flower of Maui, is the beloved familiar pink rose called by Hawaiians "rose of heaven". Pipe it with tube 104 on a number 7 nail. Pipe tube 67 leaves on wire.

MOKIHANA, Kauai's emblem. Pipe leaves on fine florists' wire. Bind the leaves together with floral tape. Pipe the fruits with tube 2.

KUKUI, the flower of Molokai, and also the state tree of Hawaii.

Insert the end of a fine florists' wire into a cone fitted with tube 2. Pull out to coat the wire for about one inch. Touch the wide end of tube 101s to the wire and pull up and out to make five tiny petals. Pipe stamens with tube 1. Dry, then tape into spray. Pipe the leaves with tube 68 on wire stems. First pipe two lobes for base of leaf, then two more lobes above them. Pull out a long slender lobe in center and brush smooth.

LEHUA HAOLE is the flower of the big island, Hawaii. Pipe fluffy red pom-pons with stiff royal icing. Pull out six spikes with tube 18 and top with tube 2 balls. Then cover with tube 233, starting at base. To make the fern-like leaves, curve a 4" florists' wire, insert in cone fitted with tube 3, and pull out to cover wire with green icing. Dry, then lay on wax paper and pipe tube 65 leaves.

SUMMER'S AT ITS BEST on the fourth of July! Bands are playing, parades are marching and all over town celebrations are being held in parks, on beaches and in back yards. Join the fun—bring one of these colorful cakes to the picnic or barbecue.

A red-white-and-blue butterfly

Start with a single-layer sheet cake and produce this brilliant butterfly.

1. Bake a 9″ x 13″ sheet cake, 2″ deep. Chill cake, then cut 2″ off one short side. Cut remaining cake in half, diagonally, and trim as shown on *Celebrate! IV* pattern. Ice the three parts thinly with white buttercream. Mold five stars in sugar, using Star candy mold. Set aside to dry. The three parts of the butterfly are decorated separately.

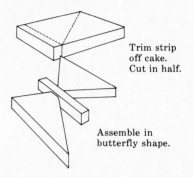

Trim strip off cake. Cut in half.

Assemble in butterfly shape.

2. Transfer *Celebrate! IV* patterns to each wing. Outline with tube 2 then fill in red and white areas with tube 18 stars. Pipe white stars on field of

flag, then surround with blue stars. Bring stars down on sides of cake. Overpipe the white stars on the blue field to make them stand out.

Cover the butterfly body with tube 16 blue stars.

3. Center the butterfly body on foil-covered cake board. Press the sugar-molded stars on top, using picture as guide. Set each wing on cake board, closely against body. Serves about twelve.

Dress up a star cake with true-blue hearts

A star-shaped cake takes on a patriotic spirit when decorated with hearts and stripes.

1. Bake a two-layer cake in Star-shaped pans. Fill, then ice smoothly. Set on foil-covered, star-shaped cake board.

2. Pattern top of cake by pressing a 2½" Heart Cutter on each point. Mark the stripes on the cake sides. On top edge of cake, starting at inner point, make a mark every half-inch. On base of cake, start at outer point and make a mark every half-inch. Connect the sets of marks to make diagonal stripes.

3. Use tube 16 to fill in patterns with stars. Outline the hearts with stars, then fill in. Outline edge of each stripe with stars and fill in. Pipe a tube 18 star border at bottom and top of cake. Push in a tall red taper and light it. Then present your patriotic masterpiece. Serves ten, generously.

Wave the glorious colors on a sheet cake

Bring this star-spangled cake to the picnic. It's quick to decorate, inspiring to view, and very easy to serve.

1. Sugar mold seven white stars and fourteen blue stars in Star candy molds. When stars are thoroughly dry, brush with egg white and sprinkle with edible glitter.

2. Bake a 9" x 13" two-layer sheet cake. Fill and ice with buttercream and place on a foil-covered cake board. Pipe a tube 18 bottom shell border. Transfer *Celebrate! IV* pattern to cake top and pipe design with tube 16 stars. Attach white sugar stars with dots of icing.

3. Divide long sides of cake into fourths, shorter sides into thirds. Drop a tube 14 drape from point to point. Add tube 14 loops and stars at points where drapes meet. Attach blue sugar stars with dots of icing. Serves 24 patriotic guests.

Quick & Pretty

Quick & Pretty

A fairytale wedding ornament

YOU CAN CREATE this beautiful bride and her dashing Prince Charming—with the help of Wilton People Molds and gum paste. These never-before molds form man, woman, ten-year old and five-year old child figures, so you can model an entire wedding party if you like, complete with flower girl and ring bearer—all in proportion.

With the molds comes a colorful booklet that shows you just how to mold the figures and dress them in whatever costume you desire.

Before starting, study the People Mold booklet. Then enjoy the adventure of making your own romantic bridal couple to adorn a fabulous wedding cake.

Mold and dress the bride

Read the directions for modeling and dressing a standing figure in the

People Mold book. Here we give you only the details that are specific to this costume. *Celebrate! IV Pattern Book* gives the pattern for skirt.

1. Drape the beautiful blue sash after the skirt has dried on the figure. Use a little *very soft* gum paste that has not been stiffened with additional sugar. Make your own pattern by cutting out a rectangle ¾″ x 4½″ from light cardboard. Make a second pattern for streamer by cutting a long triangle, 2½″ at base with each long side 7½″. Cut off 1″ from point.

Roll the soft gum paste very thin and cut the sash. Brush a little egg white around top of skirt and drape the sash around the hips. Cut the streamer. Brush egg white on skirt just below closing of sash. Pleat top of streamer and press to skirt. Arrange in graceful folds. Add the arms and the figure is almost complete.

2. The finishing touches are the most fun! Embroider the dress with tube 1, starting at hem. Pipe tube 1s hair and necklace.

Make tiny rose on end of an icing-covered wire. Hand-model petals from little balls of gum paste, attaching with egg white. Cut ⅛″ wide gum paste strips, form loops and streamers and attach to stem with egg white while still wet. When dry, secure to hand with royal icing.

3. Form a little string of gum paste into a circlet, 1″ in diameter, for crown. Dry, then trim with tube 1s. Fold a 24″ x 10″ piece of fine tulle in half to make 12″ x 10″ veil. Gather 10″ folded edge and secure to hair with royal icing. Attach crown with icing.

Mold and dress Prince Charming

Mold the figure following directions for standing figure in People Mold booklet. Legs and lower body are molded in green gum paste, other parts in flesh color. Make an extra head and upper torso to help in draping the cape.

1. Dress the figure in jacket and boots as described in booklet. Add cuffs to boot by cutting a ½″ x 2⅞″ strip, moistening long edge with egg white and attaching to boot.

2. After trimming jacket with gold strips, add the sash. Cut a ½″ x 8″ strip, apply a little egg white to shoulder and drape wet sash around figure. Secure with more egg white at right side and trim ends.

3. Cut cape from *Celebrate! IV* pattern. Roll lower edge with modeling stick 2 to make folds. Lay extra upper torso face down, form a pleat in center of cape, and place on back of extra torso. Use cotton balls to preserve folds while drying. When cape is dry, turn over and pipe royal icing fleurs-de-lis with tube 1s.

4. Pipe hair with tube 1s. Dry, then cut a ¼″ strip of gold gum paste, trim to point in front, brush egg white on head and wrap around. Trim coronet with tube 1s.

5. Cut 2½″ x ½″ strips of gum paste for cuffs. Brush one edge with egg white and attach to sleeve. When dry, trim with a ⅛″ wide gold strip. Attach cape to shoulders with small pieces of gum paste dipped in egg white. Cut a ¼″ strip for cape strap and attach. Trim strap with tube 1s design in royal icing. Make brooches for cape strap from flattened small balls of gum paste. Attach to ends of strap with egg white and impress with tube 26. Finally, trim sleeve and boot cuffs with tube 1 cornelli. Prince Charming is complete!

A Fairytale Bridal Cake

Decorate this delicately beautiful cake as a setting for the handmade bride and groom. The dainty gum paste blossoms echo the colors in their costumes.

Make trims in advance

1. The flowers are made from gum paste, using the forget-me-not and violet cutters. You will need a great many, but the cutters make them quick to do. Tint gum paste (recipe page 22), roll out very thin and cut the flowers. Lay on foam toweling and press each petal from edge to center to curl. Dry, then pipe tube 2 stamens.

Mount about 300 violets on fine florists' wire stems. Mount about 25 forget-me-nots on wire stems. Remaining flowers will form clusters.

2. Make double ring ornament for top of cake. Cut a 10″ gum paste strip, 3/8″ wide, and set on edge to form a 3″ circle. Cut an 8″ strip, 1/4″ wide and form into 2½″ circle. Dry. Trim rings with tube 1s beading and zigzags.

Cut a 4½″ circle from 1″ thick styrofoam and ice with royal icing. Pipe tube 14 fleur-de-lis around sides and edge with stars piped with same tube. Secure rings upright on this base with royal icing. Tape about two dozen wired forget-me-nots into a cluster with floral tape and insert in base behind rings.

3. Make heart bouquet for between pillars. You will need six gum paste hearts. Cut from gum paste, using 1″ heart cutter. Cut one heart, dip florists' wire in egg white and lay on heart. Dry. Cut second heart, brush first heart with egg white and join the two. Dry, then edge with tube 1 beading. Tape into spray. Ice a 3″ styrofoam half-ball. Tape wired violets into several sprays and insert into half-ball along with heart spray.

4. Make flowery base for bridal couple. Ice a 10″ styrofoam circle, 1″ thick, and edge with tube 13 shells. Make many sprays of violets by taping stems together. Insert in base, keeping flowers low in front and gradually rising to about a 3″ height in back.

Prepare the wedding cake

Bake, fill and ice the two-layer tiers—16″ round, 12″ round and 9″ hexagon. Set 16″ tier on top separator plate of Arched Pillar tier set. Insert dowel rods, clipped off level with top, to support upper tiers, then center 12″ tier. Insert dowel rods into this tier and top with a 9″ hexagon separator plate.

Make a separator plate for below top tier from heavy cardboard. Cover with pastel foil and glue on six stud plates, lining up with hexagon plate on 12″ tier. Use 5″ Grecian pillars.

Decorate the cake

1. Pipe six arches on sides of base tier. The upright columns are done with tube 32, the scrolls above with tube 18. Pipe tube 18 shells around bottom and top.

2. On 12″ tier pipe a tube 17 shell border at base. Top with tube 13 strings. Drop triple strings with tube 13 from top of tier, lining up with arches on tier below. Leave about 2½″ of space between triple strings. Edge top of tier with tube 17 shells. Edge hexagon separator plate with tube 13.

3. Pipe a mound of icing extending over top edge of 12″ tier and halfway down side, between two sets of triple strings. Press in flowers, placing larger ones in center. Attach smaller flowers on outside of mound with dots of icing.

Continue making flower clusters, six on 12″ tier and six on 16″ tier.

4. On top tier, pipe upright columns at each corner with tube 32. Add two scrolls at top of each with tube 16, then center scrolls with a tube 16 star. Using same tube, pipe a shell border at base and a star border on top edge of tier. Finish with a fleur-de-lis on each side.

Assemble the wedding cake

1. Center flower base on base plate of Arched Pillar set. Attach bridal couple by pushing wires on feet into styrofoam. Set pillars in place, then position two lower tiers on pillars.

2. Secure heart bouquet to hexagon separator plate with icing. Set 5″ pillars in position and add top tier. Pipe a mound of icing on top of tier and attach double ring ornament. This romantic masterpiece serves 208.

A dainty announcement cake

This little cake gives a hint of the splendid bridal cake to come.

1. Bake an 8″ two-layer round cake. Fill and ice with Snowwhite Buttercream. (Recipe is on page 16.)

2. Cover with Wilton Quick Fondant (page 13). Let fondant set, then mark a 4″ circle in center of cake. Outline with tube 2 beading. Working from circle out, cover entire cake with tube 1s freehand embroidery. Pipe a tube 8 ball border at bottom.

3. Make gum paste violets just as described for wedding cake above. Mount on wire stems, then group into bouquet with floral tape. Tie with a ribbon and place in center of cake. Present the bouquet to the bride-to-be. Serves twelve.

Going places

GETTING THERE is half the fun in the summer! Bake one of these cute travel cakes and have a party to send the travelers on their way.

Take the train to the city

Build this little engine of cookies and cake, and ice it in cheerful colors.

1. Cut the cookies that make the cab, using *Celebrate! IV* patterns and roll-out cookie dough (recipe, page 147). Also cut four wheels with the 3⅜" round cutter and two headlights with a 1⅜" cutter. Cut a 5" x 6½" rectangle for roof of cab. Cut the two circles to attach to side rods on wheels with the end of tube 2A.

After cookies are baked, paint them with thinned icing. Cut a 7½" length of ¼" dowel rod for side rod and paint with thinned icing. Outline stripes on cow catcher with tube 2 and fill in with thinned icing.

2. For body of engine, bake five layers in the 6" hexagon pan. Chill, then stack the layers with icing between each. Push two dowel rods through layers and clip off level with top. Ice smoothly.

3. Cut support for train from styrofoam and ice with green royal icing. Cut a 16" x 9" rectangle for base from 1" styrofoam, ice green and pat with damp sponge.

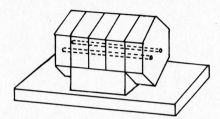

4. Assemble train with royal icing. Place supports on base, then secure cake on supports. Ice back of train. (This was the bottom of cake.) Build the cookie cab and attach the big wheels, headlights and cow catcher with royal icing. Pipe a line of icing on the base and attach strips of licorice for tracks. Pipe tube 4 beading as picture shows.

Model the smokestack from marzipan (recipe, page 23), push a thin dowel rod into it and down through cake. Add the side rod and two small cookies to wheels. Finish the scene with drop flowers. Cake serves about 15.

Float down the river...

in a homey houseboat. This leisurely craft is constructed of cake with a cookie roof.

1. Cut two rectangles, 6¾" x 3½" from cookie dough for roof. Also cut a door, 2½" x 1¼" and two or more little cookie "people". Bake the cookies, then outline the door and people with tube 1 and Color Flow icing and fill in areas. Add details with tube 1. Make tiny tube 23 drop flowers.

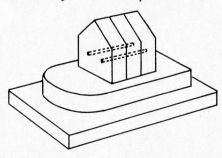

2. Bake three layers of cake in 5" square pans. Fill and stack. Run two thin dowel rods through cakes and clip off level with surface. Set cake on side and trim roof to a peak as diagram shows. Ice smoothly.

Bake a 9" x 13" x 2" cake and trim to boat shape, rounding front edges. Cut a 16" x 12" rectangle from 1" styrofoam for base and ice. Center

boat on base and ice boat. Pipe border on top edge of boat with tube 4. Set house on boat.

3. Using *Celebrate! IV* pattern, mark position of windows. Outline windows and shutters with tube 1 and fill in shutters with short strokes of tube 101s. Cut sugar cubes in half and paint with thinned icing for flower boxes. Do triangles on front of house with tube 3.

Attach roof and door. Trim roof with tube 3 string and pipe beading on top with same tube. Attach flower boxes, then add flowers and trim with tube 65s leaves. Prop people on deck with toothpicks. Push a dowel rod through the deck into base for flag pole. Attach a fine wire for "clothes line". Cut clothes and flag from paper using *Celebrate! IV* pattern and glue to line and pole.

Cut macaroni into 3″ lengths and push into deck for railing. Join with tube 3 string. Heap icing on base to resemble waves. Ready to push off! Serves about 28.

You can take it with you!

Roll along in a camper made of cake with cookie windows!

1. Bake two 12″ x 2″ square cakes and construct the camper as diagram shows. Set on a 4″ x 6″ x 1¼″ iced styrofoam block. Using *Celebrate! IV* patterns, cut bumpers, grill and windows from cookie dough. Cut four 2½″ and four 1⅜″ circles for wheels, two 1″ circles for headlights and three or more 1⅜″ circles for faces. Bodies are 2″ half-cookies. Paint cookies with thinned royal icing. Add details to faces with tube 2.

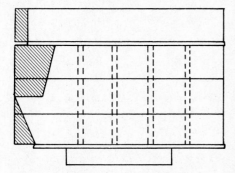

2. Coat entire camper thinly with icing. Transfer *Celebrate! IV* flower design to sides and top. Use tube 16 for all decorating. First do flower design with stars. Attach all cookies with royal icing. Outline windows with stars, then fill in entire area with yellow and white stars as pictured. Serves about 36.

Figure piping is fun!

A visit to the zoo is a lot of fun on a summer day—make the fun last longer by having a little party on the porch when you come home. Serve icy drinks and one of these wonderful zoo cakes. The children will be charmed by the figure piped animals.

Here we show two versions of the figure piping technique. The giraffes use the fill-in method and the seals are done in the upright method. Both require careful control of pressure for success—both give spectacular three-dimensional results.

Let's go to the zoo

Pipe a baby giraffe and his mother

PIPE THE BABY GIRAFFE FIRST

Though only a few hours old, this little fellow is five feet tall! Royal icing is the best for piping these fill-in method figures. Tape *Celebrate! IV* pattern to stiff board and tape wax paper over it.

1. Use tube 4 to pipe head, starting at top back with heavy pressure and moving forward to nose and lips with lighter pressure. With point of damp brush, define lips and indent eyes. Pipe ears and horns with tube 2.

Use tube 8 to pipe arched neck and torso. Flatten torso and shape with your fingers. Pipe the two legs in background with tube 3, increasing pressure to form knobby knees. Pipe forward front leg with tube 4, using heavy pressure at shoulder and decreasing pressure as you move down leg. Do the forward rear leg with tube 4, heavy pressure at top, much lighter pressure for lower leg. Shape with your fingers.

2. Pipe tail with tube 2 and add mane with tube 1. Pipe eye with tube 2. Dry thoroughly, then paint light brown spots with thinned icing. Add little black hooves.

PIPE MAMA GIRAFFE

1. Mama is piped much like baby. Use tube 4 for head, moving from back to front with heavy pressure. You will need to make several strokes to fill in area. Smooth with finger and shape eyes, lips and nostril with point of brush. Pipe neck with tube 10, using light pressure where it joins head and increasing to shoulder. Pipe torso with same tube, then shape and flatten with your finger. Pipe two legs in background with tube 4, making knobby knees.

Pipe two legs in foreground with tube 8, applying very heavy pressure at top of legs and much lighter pressure as you go down.

2. Finish by piping tube 3 horns, ears and eye. Add tail with same tube. Pipe tube 3 hooves and brush to shape. Do mane with tube 1. Dry, then paint spots with thinned icing.

DECORATE CAKE

1. Bake and ice a 9″ × 13″ × 3″ cake. Let icing set, then apply a coat of green icing on cake top for "grass". Pat with clean damp sponge. Pipe a tube 17 shell border at base, tube 16 border at top.

2. Pipe tree trunk and branches with tube 5. Pull out leaves with tube 65. Pipe tube 1 grass. Set giraffes in position on mounds of icing. Serves 24.

Pipe two playful seals

Seals are quick and fun to figure pipe. Use the recipe below for this upright figure piping.

1. Wrap a marshmallow in plastic wrap as a "leaning post" to pipe seal on rock. Starting at tail, use tube 2A and medium pressure as you go up. Increase pressure, then lighten as you pull out to tapered nose. Cut tip of cone in "V" shape to pipe front flippers. Use tube 102 to pipe the seal's back flippers.

2. Pipe second seal on wax paper the same way, bending body sharply as you approach head. Pipe beady eyes with black piping gel on both seals.

3. Coat marshmallow with royal icing for rock for seal to lean on. Pipe a number of smaller rocks. Bake and fill an 8″ × 3″ square cake. Mark curving line on top. Ice sides and top, up to line, blue. Ice rest of top beige. Do bottom bulb border with tube 5, top border with tube 2. Brush piping gel over blue area of top. Pipe the fish on the side with tube 8 and add tube 2 tails and mouths. Use piping gel for bubbles coming from fishes' mouths. Attach rocks and seals. Serves twelve guests.

FIGURE PIPING ICING

A heavy consistency icing for piping upright figures.

3 cups granulated sugar
⅔ cup water
¼ teaspoon cream of tartar
4 tablespoons meringue powder
⅔ cup lukewarm water
2¼ cups sifted confectioners' sugar

Cook first three ingredients to 234°; set aside. Beat meringue with lukewarm water until peaks form. Add confectioners' sugar slowly, then beat at medium speed until blended. Pour in cooked mixture and continue beating until peaks form. (Note: You must use a heavy-duty mixer to make this icing.)

Just-for-fun cakes

Quick & Pretty

Quick & Pretty

Quick & Pretty

MAKE ANY DAY a holiday—don't wait for a special occasion. Just call the group together and bring out a pretty cake, decorated with flair. It's an instant party!

Surprise your little leaguer...

with a cake that looks like him! One cake mix, tinted icing and just a little time is all it takes.

1. Bake two layers in oval pans. Cool, then ice cakes thinly with flesh-colored icing. Transfer *Celebrate! IV* pattern to cakes.

2. Use stiff icing to pipe the ears. Pipe a curve with tube 104, then edge it with tube 6. Dry or freeze. Outline caps, eyes, nose and mouth with tube 3. Fill in all areas with tube 16 stars. Attach ears with mounds of icing and toothpicks. Pipe strands of hair with tube 16.

Pipe blue eyes with tube 6 and flatten with fingertip. Pipe nose and button on cap with tube 8. Over-pipe mouth with tube 6 then glaze eyes with corn syrup. Serves twelve.

Sail away

A trio of colorful sailboats skim across a sheet cake. Bring this treat out after a day at the beach.

1. Bake a 9″ × 13″ × 2″ cake. Cut the boats from a small cake using the three sizes of the Boat Cutters.

2. Ice boats and edge with tube 13 shells. Cut sails and pennants from stiff paper, using *Celebrate! IV* patterns or your own. Glue to wooden skewers and insert in boats.

3. Ice the cake white. Pipe tube 16 top and bottom shell borders. Use the same tube to pipe the wavy scroll side border. (For a close-up of technique, see page 16.) Add a little blue food color to remaining icing and stir a few times for streaky effect. Swirl on top of cake. Set boats in position and bring "waves" up against their sides with a spatula.

Serves 24 with three lucky children getting the sailboats.

Welcome new neighbors

The new family on the block will feel right at home when you bring over this welcome cake decorated with a sunny Hawaiian flair.

1. Bake a 9″ × 13″ × 2″ sheet cake and ice smoothly. Set on cake board. Write message with tube 2. Pipe a tube 22 base shell border and a tube 14 top border.

2. You'll be surprised at how quickly you can pipe the lei. Sketch its rough outline on the cake with a toothpick. Tint icing in sunny colors. Pipe a tube 6 mound on this line. Use tube 233 to pull out many strands, starting at base of mound and finishing at top. Continue piping flowers close together on outline until lei looks full and fluffy. Cake serves 24.

A pretty patchwork cake

Display this showy cake after a barbecue in the back yard. It's so easy to serve—each guest receives a pre-cut decorated triangle.

1. Bake two single layers in 9″ pans from the Hexagon Tier set. Chill, then cut each cake into six triangles by slicing from corners to opposite corners. Ice each triangle with white buttercream.

2. Roll out marzipan and cut 72 little hearts with 1″ Heart Cutter. Set six iced triangles on a rack over a cookie sheet. Make a recipe of Quick Fondant (page 13), tint yellow, and pour over cakes, touching up bare spots with a spatula. (Fondant can be scraped off cookie sheet and used again.) While fondant is still soft, arrange the marzipan hearts on triangles in a neat pattern.

Tint a second recipe of Quick Fondant pink and pour over remaining iced triangles. Arrange marzipan hearts on top of each. Let fondant set, then place cakes on a 16″ cake board or tray, alternating yellow and pink. A stunning effect, achieved very simply! Serves 12.

The Hawaiian double canoe

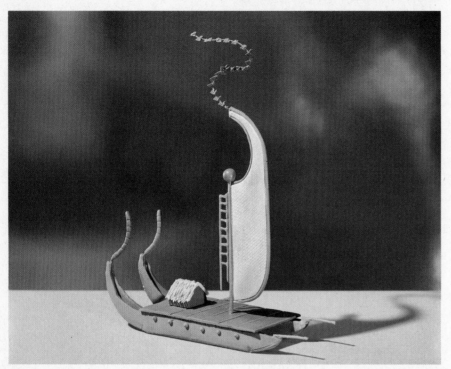

This little craft is a replica of the double canoes that carried the first Hawaiians from the Marquesas Islands in about the eighth century A.D. Boats like these were still in use for travel between the islands of Hawaii when Westerners first discovered the Hawaiian Islands. With their platform and thatched hut, they could carry as many as 50 people and their belongings.

Hawaiian traditions speak of two-way voyages in these canoes between Hawaii and Tahiti, a distance of 2000 miles of open ocean.

Archaeologists are amazed at the skill of these early navigators who could guide their craft so accurately without the use of maps, instruments, or ships with deep draught. They have concluded that the Hawaiians were expert astronomers.

The replica is made of gum paste, (recipe page 22), and the dried parts assembled with royal icing. Complete directions and patterns are in Celebrate! IV Pattern Book.

Plan a joyful celebration for First Communion day

Serve this reverent, symbolic cake at a family gathering after the church service. Your little first communicant will feel very proud.

1. Bake, fill and ice a two-layer 10″ cake. Pipe the script with tube 2. Do bottom bulb border with tube 8, top border with tube 6.

2. The figure piped grapes and the grape leaves may be done off the cake in royal icing on wax paper, or on the cake in buttercream. For each grape cluster, pipe a shell-shaped mound of icing with tube 8. Use tube 6 to pipe each grape on top of shell, starting at the tip of the cluster, and overlapping as you go to the top. If the grapes were piped in royal icing, dry, then place on cake.

Pipe the leaves with tube 70, pulling out points with an artist's brush immediately. If you are piping them directly on the cake, do them after you pipe the wheat.

3. Do the wheat by piping four curved stems with tube 2. Pipe teardrop-shaped kernels on either side and on top of stems with tube 3. Finish with long strands extending from the kernels piped with tube 1s. Add a tube 104 ribbon bow. Your celebration cake serves 14.

Good news for readers

A hearty thank you to each of the thousands of readers
who entered creative cakes in the Celebrate! IV original cake contests.
The next six pages show the winners of individual contests.

Special awards

While not Grand Prize winners, special awards are given to two of our readers for their excellence in gum paste work. Each receives a gift package consisting of the Baroque Molds, Flower Garden Cutter Set and Wilton People Molds. Their cakes are shown on page 113. The winners are:

Margaret Cornish
for her "Hardworking Executive" cake

Margaret Kemp
for her christening cake

First grand prize

A $300 gift certificate to

Mary Alice Casper

for her "Successful Farmers" cake

shown on page 109

Second grand prize

A $200 gift certificate to

Janet Chaykin

for her "Carousel" cake

shown on page 110

Third grand prize

A $100 gift certificate to

Lucille Ferguson

for her "Royal Icing Train" cake

shown on page 111

Prize winners in the Cakes for Men contest

To design a truly original cake for a man is a difficult task—but our creative readers sent in hundreds of clever ideas. Here are the winners— see two cakes awarded Honorable Mention on page 112.

First prize, the handyman

MR. STEVE SCOGLIO of Susanville, California used a variety of techniques to create this first prize-winning, humorous 12″ cake. He was very careful with details so all were crooked or tilted as an inept "do-it-yourselfer" might make them. The barbecue was cut from an 8″ square cake with the leftover cake used for the mortar tub. The birdbath is made from three sugar molded bells, trimmed and joined with royal icing. The "handyman" is figure piped with tubes 1A and 12, and brown sugar was used for sand. Bricks are piped with tube 46. Tube 233 was used to pipe grass. A gum paste plaque is attached to the side of the cake. Congratulations and a $50 gift certificate to Mr. Scoglio.

Second prize, the gourmet chef

MARGARET CORNISH of Sacramento, California created this comical second prize-winning 10″ cake with Color Flow. She put her drawing ability to good use and her workmanship is excellent on this cake. The patterns are in *Celebrate! IV Pattern Book*. Sticks are attached to the backs of the chef and animals so they stand upright. The borders are piped with tube 27. A $35 gift certificate and our congratulations to Margaret Cornish.

Third prize, the admiral

MRS. PAUL GREEN of Algona, Iowa really used her imagination for building this pontoon boat cake from a 10″ square, two jelly rolls, 2 small Wonder Molds and a 14″ x 16″ base cake. She also shows how a novelty ornament can be used tastefully. Patterns for the royal icing fence are in *Celebrate! IV Pattern Book*. The pontoons are made with the jelly rolls and small Wonder Molds. The Salty Skipper completes the scene. Congratulations and a $25 gift certificate to Mrs. Green.

Prize winners in the Cakes for Teens contest

Teen-agers, with their varied interests, love a cake made especially with them in mind. These winning cakes will inspire all of us when decorating cakes for this active age group. Two cakes winning Honorable Mention are on page 112.

First prize, successful farmers

MARY ALICE CASPER of Wilsonville, Nebraska made this first prize-winning 9″ x 13″ cake for two boys who bought a piece of land and started raising cattle. It's a very clever recreation of a scene, using real ingenuity for the patterns and construction of the windmill. Her cake was a real compliment to the boys. All patterns for the Color Flow pieces are in *Celebrate! IV Pattern Book*. Water tank is a 4″ round piece of cake with blue-tinted piping gel for water. A $50 gift certificate and our congratulations to Mary Alice Casper for her creative cake.

Second prize, number one!

ALFREDO MARR of Camp Lejeune, North Carolina won second prize with his soccer champs cake. It shows a good use of shaped cakes, with the base cake as the "field." It uses a 12″ x 18″ cake for the base, a ball cake for the soccer ball and an 8″ square cake cut in half, stacked and carved for the shoe. Green-tinted coconut is sprinkled on the top of the cake. Thank you and a $35 gift certificate to Mr. Marr.

Third prize, a pennant!

PAT WILLIAMS of Inver Grove Heights, Minnesota made this third prize-winning pennant cake that again shows teen interest in soccer. She also shows her skill in using the Color Flow technique. It is made from an 11″ x 15″ cake by cutting off two triangular pieces 2¾″ wide at base and 15″ long and placing them back against the cake to form the pennant shape. Patterns are in *Celebrate! IV Pattern Book*. This cake can be easily adapted to represent the pennant of your teen's favorite team. Congratulations and a $25 gift certificate to Pat Williams.

Prize winners in the *Cakes for Children* contest

Children like cakes that are fun, original and made just for them. Hundreds of clever, funny and cute cakes were entered by our creative readers. These prize winners will delight any child and give you new ideas for creating children's cakes. Two cakes winning Honorable Mention are shown on page 113.

First prize, carousel cake

JANET CHAYKIN of Davis, California created this darling first prize-winning carousel cake using Color Flow to make the horses, top mirrors, side mirrors and tent. She used a great deal of ingenuity in designing and creating this happy cake. The carousel is built around an 8″ cake. It is trimmed with shells and scrolls made with star tubes. Silver dragees are used to create the "mirrors". Complete patterns and instructions are in *Celebrate! IV Pattern Book*. Gum paste can substitute for Color Flow when making the pieces for this cake. Congratulations and a $50 gift certificate to Janet Chaykin.

Second prize, calico cat

PATTI JO TEEL of Hope, New Mexico won second prize with her adorable cat cut from a 9″ x 13″ x 2″ cake. The pattern is in *Celebrate! IV Pattern Book*. The cat is filled in with tube 16 stars, using different colors to achieve an interesting patchwork effect. Tube 10 was used to pipe the eyes, nose and outline. The mouth was piped with tube 7. A $35 gift certificate and our congratulations to Patti Jo Teel for her original cake.

Third prize, flower train

SUSAN HANES of Virginia Beach, Virginia won third prize for this 11″ x 15″ cake that uses Little Loafers as train cars. This pretty cake is well-designed and executed skillfully. Susan made many varieties of flowers from royal icing to trim the train and base cake. The track is piped with tube 4. The cars are edged with tube 15 and windows piped with tube 2. The shell borders are made with tubes 17 and 19. Congratulations and a $25 gift certificate to Susan Hanes for her cute cake.

Hundreds of occupations—including nearly every pursuit from aeromechanic to zookeeper—were honored in the original and creative entries we received from our readers. So many were intriguing that deciding on the finalists was extremely difficult for the judges. Here are the winners. A cake winning Honorable Mention is on page 113.

First prize, royal train

LUCILLE FERGUSON of Urbana, Illinois created this first prize-winning royal icing train cake. Her workmanship is excellent and the design unique. The train is piped on net with tube 1 using the patterns in *Celebrate! IV Pattern Book*. It is set on a 12″ square cake with a 6″ wide semi-circle cut from the bottom to form a bridge. Swans and cattails piped with royal icing are added under the bridge in the piping gel used for "water." The cake is trimmed with tube 1 cornelli and tube 13 shells. Our congratulations and a $50 gift certificate to Mrs. Ferguson.

Second prize, an Air Force symbol

CAPTAIN AND MRS. DOUGLAS WOOD, stationed with the U.S. Air Force in Germany, won second prize for the cake they created for two retiring Air Force sergeants. The Color Flow designs are especially well done. The patterns are in *Celebrate! IV Pattern Book*. Top and bottom shell borders were added with tube 27. Thank you and a $35 gift certificate to Captain and Mrs. Wood.

Third prize, fireman's hat

ALWYNE KLEMENKO of Stony Brook, New York won third prize with her fireman's hat cake. She made this unique cake by trimming a 9″ x 13″ and a Wonder Mold cake. After icing it red, she brushed it with red-tinted piping gel for a shiny look. The plaque on the front is gum paste, dried over a rolling pin. Tube 14 lines are piped down the Wonder Mold and tube 14 shell borders are piped around the brim of the hat. Congratulations and a $25 gift certificate to Alwyne Klemenko.

Honorable Mention Contest Winners

So many inspired cake ideas were submitted by our readers to the four contests that it was difficult to choose the winners. In every contest we awarded at least one Honorable Mention because so many cakes were clever and unique. They are shown on this page and the next. There are even two special awards shown on the next page.

Tennis Racket

BETTY BARNES of Statesboro, Georgia was awarded an Honorable Mention in the Cakes for Teens Contest for her well-executed tennis racket cake. She made her pattern by trac-

ing a tennis racket, used a 3" ball mold for the tennis ball and covered the entire cake with stars. The strings were piped with tube 2. Roses and daisies were added for a lovely feminine touch. Congratulations and a $10 gift certificate to Betty Barnes.

Race Car

JUDI BURCH of Fort Worth, Texas won an Honorable Mention in the Cakes for Teens contest for her race car cake. A major feature is that although it is a cut-out cake, it completely utilizes all pieces of the cake. To create it, she uses a 9" x 13" cake, cuts a curved section from one end and places it upside down at the opposite end of the cake for the back of the car. A 1" x 2" oval piece is cut out of the center of the cake and the pieces used for the driver's seat and windshield. (Diagram of construction is in *Celebrate! IV Pattern Book*.) The car is decorated with stars and cookie wheels. Congratu-

lations and a $10 gift certificate to Judi Burch for her unique shaped cake.

Golf Ball and Golfer

MARY COURTNEY BENNETT of West Sedona, Arizona received an Honorable Mention in the Cakes for Men Contest for her humorous golf ball cake. Her use of a novelty ornament is excellent. The base is 11" x 15", the golf ball baked in the Ball Pan. A funnel is used for the tee and the Dapper Duffer ornament completes the scene. A $10 gift certificate and our congratulations to Mrs. Bennett.

White-faced Hereford

JANINE MAGRATH of Seymour, Connecticut was awarded an Honorable Mention in the Cakes for Men Contest for her hereford cake. She made a Color Flow plaque and when dry, painted the hereford face on it with tinted piping gel. The plaque is placed on a 10" cake and surrounded

with a rope border. Other Color Flow pieces depicting cattle in various poses are attached around the side of the cake. Patterns are in *Celebrate! IV Pattern Book*. A rope border is piped around the top of the cake and a shell border around the base. Congratulations and a $10 gift certificate to Mrs. Magrath for her very artistic cake.

Tunnel and Train

MRS. TENA ANDERSON of Tacoma, Washington was awarded Honorable Mention in the Cakes for Children contest for her tunnel and train cake. Tena created her unique cake by using an 8″ two-layer cake and placing it on a large rectangular board. She then cut a tunnel partway into the side of the cake and did the same directly across from it so the tunnel appeared to go through the cake. Tube 47 was used to make the tracks and tunnel wall. The bor-

ders are piped with star tubes. Roses, candles and flags adorn the top and a few trees added near the track. A small toy train is placed on the track for the finishing touch. Congratulations and a $10 gift certificate to Mrs. Anderson for her very creative cake.

Clown Cake

VIRGINIA MCMACKEN of St. Louis, Michigan received Honorable Mention in the Cakes for Children contest for her clown cake. The design and construction is very creative and the workmanship excellent. Virginia baked an 8″ one-layer cake for the clown's collar and a cake in the ball pan for his head. The hat and ears are pieces of cardboard that have been cut, shaped and then iced. Hair is piped with tube 234, eyes and nose are made with large round tubes. The mouth is made with tube 57. Tube 127 was used to make the

double neck ruffles. Congratulations and a $10 gift certificate to Virginia McMacken for her cute, jolly cake design.

Carpenter's Box

STELLA PYRTEK of Fords, New Jersey won Honorable Mention in the Cakes Honoring Occupations contest for her realistic carpenter's box cake. The tools are made of Color Flow (patterns provided in *Celebrate! IV Pattern Book*). The box itself is made from an 11″ x 15″ cake. The cake was cut in half to form two 7½″ x 11″ layers. Then a 1½″ wide strip was cut from the long edge of each to create the top edges of the box. She added sides and handle made of iced cardboard. Stella placed tools in box and added an empty box of nails. Thank you and a $10 gift certificate to Stella Pyrtek for her inventive cake idea.

Special Awards for Excellence in Gum Paste Work

MARGARET CORNISH of Sacramento, California hand-modeled the "hardworking executive" on this delightful cake. Congratulations to Mrs. Cornish for her extremely creative cake.

MARGARET KEMP of Queensland, Australia created this charming, well-executed christening cake, covered with rolled fondant and trimmed with gum paste figures and flowers. Congratulations to Mrs. Kemp.

WE WISH TO THANK the hundreds of our reader friends who have taken the time to share with us their decorating experiences—their likes, dislikes, serious interest and proud achievements. All are valuable to us. Our very special thanks for your many compliments. They are a great source of satisfaction to all of us. Now we would like to know what you most enjoy in this book, and also what you find less inspiring and helpful. So please keep writing to let us know what *you* are doing, what techniques you have found to make decorating easier, what ideas you believe others might find profitable. *Please note that we have a new location* and send your letters to Diane Kish, Reader's Editor, Wilton Book Division, 1603 South Michigan Avenue, Chicago, Illinois 60616. KEEP WRITING. We want Celebrate! to be *your* book.

Thanks for writing

Decorating Hints

BARBARA HORTON of Lowton, Ok., gives a time-saving hint. She writes, "My husband cut lots of triangles from a roll of parchment paper, rolled them around a dowel rod and placed them in an empty paper towel cardboard roll with a long split. This is used as a cone dispenser for busy decorating days."

GERTRUDE NEGRI of Danbury, Conn. says, "Instead of using brown sugar for 'sand,' I toast coconut crisp and put it in a blender or roll it with a rolling pin. It's delicious and looks just like sand."

MRS. DONALD KEPPLE of Avon, Ill., says to keep a separator plate from lifting off the icing on the cake, she uses a piece of plastic wrap under the plate. She also includes a card with a wedding cake telling how to cut it.

SHARON NIESLANIK of Glenwood Springs, Colo., writes, "I have converted my old portable dishwasher into an ideal decorating island. The pull-out trays are handy. The island can be set in the middle of the kitchen floor and walked around for ease in decorating."

MARIAN GIBNEY of York, Pa., writes, "I have found that many people like the idea of having something to keep as a memento of an important event, so I try to put an ornament or figurine of some sort on each cake."

DONNA MAE BRIGGS of Orange, Texas, has discovered a way of making a deep red color without bitterness. Mix 1 tablespoon cocoa powder and 2 tablespoons red liquid food color. Add to buttercream icing until you achieve a shade slightly lighter than the one you want. Make several hours ahead, the color deepens as it ages.

RUTH GENTZ of Earlville, Iowa, gives this proven method for baking a level cake. "Always pin wet terrycloth strips around your pan before baking. Cakes will always rise to the top of the pan level if the pan is filled half full."

LYNN HINNERS of Montgomery, Ill. says she uses left over buttercream to make flowers and freezes them. Then she always has an assortment for decorating a cake quickly. You can do the same thing with left over royal icing. Store them in a covered container.

Transporting Cakes

MRS. JOHN WALLEWEIN of Sanhurst, Mont., puts a damp towel in a pan that is a size larger than the cake plate and places the cake in it to keep it from sliding. Then she sets it on 3" foam in a station wagon.

MRS. WAYNE PLAGMAN of Irwin, Iowa, places a damp paper towel under the cake plate in a cardboard box and covers it with plastic wrap.

Here is the way we have carried tier cakes hundreds of miles—safely. Separate the tiers by removing pillars. Carve a depression in a 3" or 4" thick piece of soft foam the exact size of the separator plate or base plate. Set the tiers in these depressions.

More Helpful Hints

Here's a real time-saving tip from MRS. NORMA PETIT of Old Orchard Beach, Maine. She says, "On several occasions I have taped a smaller size tube right over a larger tube already on a filled bag."

Another way is to use a coupler. Take off one tube, screw on another.

MRS. C. W. YANCER of Phoenix, Arizona writes, "I had a grease problem with tubes and bags when using buttercream icing. Solution—I made a net bag and run all pieces through the dishwasher."

RUBY KAZLAUCKAS of Escondido, Calif., gives good advice for any decorator. "I stress the real importance of reading instructions carefully and practicing constantly. Practice is the only way to develop a 'feel' for what is right for each decorator."

Here's some advice from BRENDA PERKINS of Pearl City, Hawaii. "I'd like to encourage more decorators to enter the cake decorating contests in their area. They're lots of fun. You'll get new ideas from other decorators and make new friends!"

MRS. D. M. ANTCZAK of Yorktown, Va., gives advice for beginning decorators. "Don't over-criticize your efforts and lose the fun of your hobby. Relax and enjoy. Your family won't notice and will love you more for it. They can eat your 'goofs'."

More advice for beginners comes from MRS. NANCY HAGGARTY of N. Kingstown, R. I. She tells her students "they must have patience and be willing to give lots of time and practice towards rewards that will be boundless."

MRS. GARY YOUNG of Chas, W. Va., has found that "some of the compliments I receive on my cakes are much more rewarding than the money I get, especially from the children. Also, I enjoy donating cakes . . . it's a rewarding feeling."

C. HUETT of Parma, Idaho, gives the following decorating tip. "Make small bows from nylon net, rub them with egg white and sprinkle with sugar. They make cute trims to add to the cake. Attach them with toothpicks. The color of the net should harmonize with the cake."

Here's a suggestion for a baby christening cake from MRS. FERRIS FOSTER of Shreveport, La. "Mold a sugar egg and carve it out to look like a cracked egg. Put a baby figure in it and place it on top of the cake."

DEBRA GRISTE of Memphis, Tenn., uses tinted white corn syrup to make a lake on the top of the cake.

MRS. ROY MILLER of St. Joseph, Mo., has a good idea for those who serve wedding cakes. "Prepare a cloth that will fit in a plastic bag about 6" long and 10" wide. Wet cloth in warm water, wring it out and fold in thirds. Place it in the bag. When cutting the cake, slip the knife between the folds of the cloth to wipe it. This keeps hands and knife clean."

Here is an interesting idea from CAROLYN BLURTON of Brownstown, Ill. "Our customers like our little cakes for birthdays. We make a small one just for the child. Then the big cake is served to the guests and the birthday child has his own cake."

JAN RODGERSON of Flint, Mich., has a time-saving tip for other decorators. She writes, "I always add a little oil to my cake mixes. I keep this in an empty plastic detergent bottle. It's easy to just give a squeeze instead of trying to pour into a measuring spoon from a drippy bottle."

C. LYONS of Hialeha, Fla., uses this method for getting a moist cake when using a cake mix. "When using a cake mix I usually add a small amount of fruit cocktail to the batter. It adds moisture to the cake and there is not enough fruit to disturb the smoothness of the cake."

EVELYN FISHER of Grand Island, Neb., gives her solution to the problem of removing Color Flow pieces from wax paper without breaking them. She says, "Do the Color Flow piece as usual and when time to remove it, use a piece of thread and ease it under the edge of the piece, working it back and forth with a sawing motion. Work it all the way under and it will be very easy to lift off. On larger pieces, work from several sides until it is loosened."

Tips on Cakes and Icings

To keep her cakes from sticking in the pans, MRS. DENNIS RICHARDS of Central City, Neb., puts corn flakes in the blender until powdery fine. Then after greasing the pan with vegetable shortening, she dusts it with the crumbs. The cake never sticks and she says she has had real success using this with 3-D pans.

NATALIE THOMAS of Lincolnville, Maine, says that by using hot water instead of milk in buttercream icing the product will keep much longer.

If the cake sticks in the pan, MRS. OLEY DOTY of Corning, N.Y. gives this advice. "Quickly run the bottom of the pan over the gas flame of the top burner, just enough to warm it. The cake will come out easily."

MRS. CONNIE WOOD of Woodstock, Ga., sends in this hint. "When trying a new cake recipe, use some of the batter for a cupcake for yourself. That way you can taste it for yourself. The same thing goes for icing."

Questions and Answers

MRS. JO JANET MORSE of Cahokia, Ill., would like to know what type of cake mix to use in shaped pans.

We recommend that a firm cake batter, such as pound cake be used for all 3-D pans.

EARL HALEY of Oklahoma City, Oklahoma, asked to see 50 state cakes for civic occasions.

In The Wilton Way of Cake Decorating, Volume Two, there is a spectacular 50 States Cake adorned with the flowers of all 50 states. There are also ideas for making cakes for each state.

CHRISTINE DUNN of North Adams, Mass. asks where she can get colored foil to cover cake boards.

This foil can be obtained at a florist or florist supply shop.

BERYL LEVEY of Forest Hills, N.Y. asks, "How far in advance can a cake be made and still be fresh? Will a refrigerated, decorated cake look as good as a freshly decorated cake?"

A cake can be made and decorated in advance and refrigerated for no more than two days. It will still look as pretty as it was when just decorated.

Freezing a decorated cake is somewhat risky. We recommend freezing only in an emergency. Baked, un-iced layers freeze well.

MRS. M. F. SANDERSON of Morris Plains, N.J., asks, "Is there any easy way to cut 3-D cakes?"

To cut a 3-D cake, slice it in half from top to bottom. Lay one half down on the cut surface and slice it into pieces. Cut the other half the same way.

MRS. SOLAND of Shelton, Wash., would like to see some things that a pre-teen girl can do to start learning cake decorating.

On pages 16 through 21 there is a section that covers the basics of decorating. It's perfect for a beginning decorator or as a "brush-up course."

JONATHAN MOYER of Valparaiso, Ind., asks why the patterns are not included in Wilton books.

The patterns we provide for our books are very numerous, and the printing cost for full color Wilton books is very high. Instead, we provide them in a convenient folder so it is easy to remove the pages to trace the patterns. All patterns are full size with nothing printed on the back and are clearly drawn. There is a handy index in the front of the folder. In this way, we are able to keep down the cost of the book and we can show more beautiful, large, full-color pictures of cakes.

SUZANNE OWEN of Ft. Lee, Va. asks for a substitution for Grayslake gelatin in recipes.

Knox or any other unflavored gelatin is a satisfactory substitute.

LYNN GASTON of Selma, Al. wants to know how the larger tubes, such as 127 and 234, are attached to the decorating bag.

We would use a 16" bag with a Quick-change Coupler.

MRS. STELLA IANULY of Bridgeport, Conn. asks, "Do you have anything on candy clay flowers?"

Candy clay, another name for gum paste, is covered very thoroughly in The Wilton Way of Cake Decorating, Volume Two and in The Wilton Way of Making Gumpaste Flowers. See page 37 in this book also.

MRS. KATHLEEN TROISI of Enterprise, Al. wrote saying she would like to see instructions on how to design your own cakes.

Mr. Wilton gives ideas in "Commonsense for Cake Decorators".

MRS. VICKY MANNING of Asheville, N.C. asks, "How high should each layer of a cake be?"

Most of our cake layers are 2" high. 1¾" layers are also acceptable.

MILDRED MITCHELL of Uniontown, Pa. writes, "How do you get buttercream icing not to break off when doing string work?"

When using buttercream icing for string work, add 1 teaspoon of light corn syrup per cup of icing. This will give it more elasticity.

MRS. RICHARD WESNNER of Whitestone, N.Y. wants to know how to handle Color Flow.

We always suggest that Color Flow pieces be completely dry before handling them. Also to handle them with extreme care. On pages 64 and 65 we show a new method of making Color Flow designs on gum paste backings so they are much more sturdy.

Success Story

How does a Denton, Texas mother of seven children spend her leisure time?

If the mother is Gail Schultz, wife of Captain Bob Schultz, American Airlines' Chief Pilot at its Fort Worth based Flight Academy, the answer is easy. After she supervises the activities of six girls and one boy (ages 8 to 18), and handles the job of managing the family's fourteen room home, she is free to operate a business she thoroughly enjoys—The Cake Décor Shop at 909 Sunset. The Cake Décor Shop supplies "everything for the cake decorator", stays open six days a week and offers an impressive range of classes in the increasingly popular art of cake decorating. Gail is the first to admit that all of this could never be done without the complete cooperation of the seven Schultz children and an unusually understanding husband.

Gail became interested in cake decorating in 1968. She took the Wilton-method course at the local J. C. Penney store in 1973, has constantly engaged in a program of self-teaching, using many of the Wilton books and has taken many classes to learn new techniques.

Like many dedicated decorators who wish to share the pleasure of cake decorating with others, Gail decided early in her career that she wanted to teach. Accordingly, with the full support of Bob and all seven children, her first combination retail store and class room was opened in Denton on March 1, 1976.

Modest beginning proves a sound approach

The approach to the new venture was cautious, but carefully planned. Starting out with a total of 750 square feet in an outlying section of Denton, approximately 350 feet was alloted to the display and sale of merchandise, the remainder used for teaching and storage. This initial operation was set up as a proprietorship and capitalized at $6,200. The store was set up to fulfill two functions: 1) teaching the art and, 2) selling "everything for the cake decorator." Both Gail and Bob planned the physical design and both worked on achieving it. Of the initial $6,200 capital outlay, allocations of money were made roughly as follows:

Merchandise for resale	$4,000
Store fixtures	600
Equipment (electric mixer, cash box and small fixtures)	400
Prepaid insurance	120
Prepaid rent	470
Sales tax in escrow	150
Telephone	65
Advertising	250
Supplies (bags, stationery, related items)	125
	$6,180

Following these start-up costs, expenses averaged about $690 a month. These did not include an accurate estimate of the labor put in by Gail and Bob, but did include all other contracted expenses. All decorators contemplating the establishment of such an operation should benefit by this planned approach and be certain that initial working capital is completely adequate to meet the needs of operating for the first twelve to eighteen months.

With this assurance of success, Gail—again assisted by a willing husband—decided to expand. The importance of *location* was now more fully realized and experience had been gained. After nearly six months of systematically searching for the right location, the decision was made to move to 909 Sunset—directly across the street from the bustling Denton Center. The new shop was opened on Monday, after closing of the original shop on the previous Friday.

The present store provides about 1200 square feet of space. 700 square feet makes up the merchandise selling area. Again, Bob Schultz, aided by Bill Wilson, a talented

friend, did most of the carpentry, painting and general remodelling of the space. Because the store had previously been a dress shop, some built-in fixtures were converted into attractive display cases. Indirect lighting was added to show off items to full advantage. The free-standing island shelf displays were purchased from a dealer in used store displays and then completely refinished. Overhead spotlights were installed. Industrial carpeting was used to cover all the selling area space and the decorating-classroom was tiled for easy maintenance.

With more space available, more items were displayed. Accordingly, the estimated cost of the present inventory was boosted to about $8,200.

In the new location, an electronic cash register was added to provide a more accurate record of all sales and a high-visibility electric sign was also purchased to attract the attention of nearby traffic. These one-time expenditures amounted to approximately $1,300, money well spent! The monthly budget in the new location is approximately $860, up from $690 in the smaller store. Sales, however, have more than made up for the increase.

Gail finds the local newspaper a very productive medium, but she also uses many other techniques to attract prospective students, who later become local customers for

ABOVE: *Decorated display cakes show customers what can be done.*
FAR LEFT: *Island displays often act as "silent salesmen".*

products. Two to three times a week she is called on to give demonstrations on cake decorating to interested groups. This she does willingly on a low key, business-like basis. She makes no charge for the demonstration. Her proven technique is to bring the cake to the meeting, decorate it and then donate the decorated cake to be raffled. She distributes cards, answers questions about classes and leaves without fanfare. Gail considers the demonstration a success, if it results in bringing one new student to the Cake Décor Shop classes. Normally it brings two, and frequently more. The Cake Décor Shop owns a copy of Wilton's newest film, *The Art of Cake Decorating*, and frequently makes special arrangements to show this to interested groups.

Five different classes held

To accommodate students at various skill levels, five different classes are taught throughout the year. These are: Beginners, Advanced, Gum Paste, Australian and English. Classes are scheduled during the day, early evening and Saturdays. The retail shop itself is open six days a week from 10 a.m. to 5 p.m.

Gail herself (and more recently the second oldest of the Schultz daughters, *Kim*) takes classes from expert decorator-teachers around the country, in order to learn new techniques and foreign methods.

Occasional special assignments, too

Gail Schultz never misses interesting opportunities in the decorating field. Accordingly, when Shirley Cothron (Miss America of 1975) became the bride of Mr. Richard Barrett shortly after Gail's first shop was opened, Gail welcomed the chance to make the wedding cake. More than one thousand attended the reception. Since the Wedding and Groom's cakes were designed to serve more than twelve hundred

people no guest was slighted!

While the new Cake Décor Shop has been open only since January, 1977, growth has been steady and profits are rising. A line of deluxe candy ingredients has been added, and the complete selection of cake decorating equipment continues to please a growing number of loyal customers. Gail continues to handle the teaching and inventory control of decorating items, Kim—second-oldest of the Schultz daughters—is rapidly becoming a proficient decorator and assistant to her mother, two part-time employees help assure good customer service at all times, and Bob, when he is not flying thirty-five thousand feet above some part of America, takes care of the books. Everyone seems to find the Cake Décor Shop all fun, with no drudgery.

ABOVE: *Mrs. Richard Barrett (Miss America, 1975) Gail and Mr. Barrett*

Decorating for Profit

"HOW CAN I GET STARTED in a decorating business of my own?" "Can you tell me how much it costs to open a shop in my home?" "My husband is just two years from retirement, and then we are going to open a decorating store of our own ... how do we start?" "What license do I need to operate my own decorating shop?" "Friends tell me I'm selling my cakes too cheap... how much should I be charging?" "What is the best way to get new customers?"

Almost word for word, these questions have been directed to *Celebrate!* so frequently there is no doubt that many decorating enthusiasts want answers. Members of the *Celebrate!* staff talked to decorators in various sections of the country who have their own businesses. Here are some of their suggestions.

Decide on your type of business
First, decide on the type of decorating business that suits your situation best. The alternatives are many. You can, as many do, work from your house, taking orders for wedding and party cakes and supplementing the family income by working at your own pace. You can also arrange (after the proper zoning regulations are met and health authority licenses are obtained) to add what amounts to *specific use* business space to your home, and then sell both decorated cakes and cake decorating products. When this is done, the local board of health and the local department with jurisdiction over building *should be consulted before any work is started.* Few communities have precisely the same regulations.

Should you plan to make use of existing space in your home, the advice of those who have already done this is to plan on providing a minimum of 400 to 600 square feet for your working and sales operation. Plan for growth.

Shopping center locations desirable
If your plans for entering one or more areas of the cake decorating business are more ambitious, the next step is to look for suitable commercial space. The first consideration should be a location where people come with regularity. Traffic is important! Decorators in many sections of the country have had their best experience choosing space either in or immediately adjacent to thriving shopping centers. Parking is important.

Choose the space to suit your need
In most cases decorators who have taken commercial space have utilized it for two purposes: 1) teaching courses and, 2) selling the products cake decorators use. Many such operations have been set up in all parts of the United States. Most appear to be doing well, some even report sales in the six-figure bracket!

First, take all the time you need to choose the right location. It may take weeks—or months! Second, plan with care. If you do sign a lease for space, try to commit yourself for just one year. Everyone gains knowledge during the first year. Also try to avoid leases that call for the payment of a percentage of your gross income.

Be practical on use of space
Those who been most successful in teaching-selling operations have started small and expanded as need dictated. *Before you commit any money* for rent, construction, fixtures, personnel or merchandise— try to work out a realistic projection of costs and income for the first year. Try to estimate as accurately as possible how much it is going to cost to put teaching-selling space into the shape you would like to see it. Teaching areas are frequently tiled; selling areas are often carpeted. Check these costs. As a guide for your planning, many successful operations utilize one thousand to fourteen hundred square feet of space, with roughly sixty percent of this area devoted to display and selling and the remainder to classroom and storage. Try to estimate the cost of your beginning stock of merchandise accurately, too. The more frequently you have items in stock when the customer asks for them, the more repeat customers you will have.

If you intend to offer merchandise for sale five and one-half or six days a week, and also propose to hold some classes at night, then additional help may be needed. Also, put some designated value on your own time. In setting up your class schedule, too, be as realistic as possible. Best to be prepared to offer what is wanted.

Thinking of selling cakes only?
A number of successful businesses have been run on a baking-and-decorating only basis. Again, a sound study of the market for wedding and party cakes in your locality should be made. Baking equipment, even though purchased used, is still rather expensive, and your potential customers should be prepared to pay what many may think is a high price—possible ninety cents to a dollar or more per serving for a wedding cake.

A final word on selling prices
There is no definitive answer to the question "how much should I charge?" *Celebrate!*'s information from decorators throughout the country is most revealing. For wedding cakes, some charge thirty-five cents per serving, others fifty, still others seventy and some ninety-five. Check what the quality bakeries in your area charge and do not hesitate to charge a price that is in line with the commercial baker's prices.

Decorators often have a tendency to under-charge. Again, be realistic and ask a fair price for your cost of materials and time! If old customers do not agree with your price schedule, develop new ones. Give demonstrations and donate the cake you decorate to the cause of the group. Or work on a modified "party plan" and decorate for a group in the interest of selling future lessons or product or both. Do not underestimate the value of your time—and put a realistic price on the expertise you have achieved!

Celebrate!

SEPTEMBER/OCTOBER...let's get together

Decorating
directions
on page 134

120

Treats to take to school

SCHOOL DAYS! Brighten them by sending little treats for the class—easy to eat and quick to do. These cupcakes and cookies are perfect for an autumn school party, or even as a special after-school snack.

Harvest cupcakes

A tray of golden ears of corn and bunches of grapes looks so tempting! Both start the same way, with egg cupcakes. Bake the cakes in the Egg Minicake pan, then decorate. One cake mix makes 24 half-egg shapes.

DECORATE THE BUNCHES OF GRAPES
Starting at the tip of the cluster, and smaller end of cake, pipe the grapes with tube 12 bulbs, overlapping as you go toward the top. Pipe a tube 11 stem and add tube 70 leaves.

DECORATE THE EARS OF CORN
Starting at the smaller end of the cake, pipe the rows of kernels with tube 353. Do the center row first, then fill in on either side of it.

Pipe long tube 70 leaves and add a tube 11 stem.

It's the Sesame Street gang!*

Here they are—Big Bird, Cookie Monster, the Count, Oscar the Grouch, Ernie and Bert—brought to life as cookies. Just mix your favorite cookie dough or use the recipe on page 147. Cutters impress a design on the dough as they cut the shapes, so it's easy to trim the cookies with tube 2 and bright icing. They'll be the talk of the school!

Smiling sunflowers

All the children will be cheered by these sunflowers, each growing in a personalized pot.

1. Pour cake batter into ice cream cones, filling about two-thirds up the sides, and bake. One cake mix will fill about 24 cones. Swirl chocolate icing on the tops and pipe green star borders with tube 15. Pipe each child's name with tube 2.

2. Cut cookies with the largest Daisy Cutter. Cut an equal number with a 1⅜" round cutter. Lay daisy cookies on popsicle sticks to bake.

3. Pipe a tube 70 leaf on each petal of the daisy cookies and press round cookies on top. Pipe bright eyes and a smile on each with tube 2. Paint stick with thinned icing. When dry, push each flower into its pot. A double treat of cookies and cake!

Let's have a party!

Quick & Pretty

AUTUMN IS PARTY TIME! And everyone loves a party. Bake some tasty Halloween treats for the children and a drum set for the teenagers. Serve with punch or soft drinks and the party has begun!

Scary cupcakes for Halloween

Top some cupcakes with Halloween picks you make yourself from gum paste. They are easy to do—the picks can be made in advance.

1. Make a recipe of gum paste following directions on page 22. Tint small pieces orange, green and black, leaving another small piece untinted. Roll out and cut around *Celebrate! IV* patterns with a sharp knife. Dry.

2. When dry, attach pieces with dots of royal icing. Add leaves and small pumpkins to large pumpkins and ghosts. Dry thoroughly.

3. Bake cupcakes, swirl with icing and insert picks. Serve at a spooky Halloween party.

A drum set for a teens' get-together

A teen-agers' party wouldn't be complete without their favorite music. So add to the festive mood with this drum set cake. Write the name of their favorite musical group or the school name on the bass drum.

1. Make styrofoam base for bass drum. Use a piece of 4″ styrofoam 12″ long, and 4″ high. Using a 10″ round pan, trace a curve on the long side of the styrofoam, leaving 1″ showing at the bottom. Cut the curve out, then trim the sides at an angle using the picture as a guide. Cover with foil.

2. Make gum paste cymbal using re-cipe on page 22. Cut a 6″ circle from light cardboard and remove a wedge. Tape edges together to create a drying form for cymbal. Roll out gum paste and cut a 6″ circle, remove a wedge and attach edges with egg

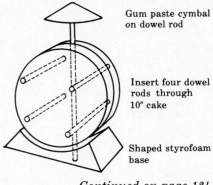

Gum paste cymbal on dowel rod

Insert four dowel rods through 10″ cake

Shaped styrofoam base

Continued on page 134

Let's get together...

**Cakes for
Autumn evenings
spent with friends**

for a game of cards

Treat your friends like royalty with clever face card cakes in every suit.

1. Bake a set of Grand Slam cakes, using a single cake mix for all four. Ice in buttercream, then pour Quick Fondant over cakes (recipe, page 13). Cover four standard size marshmallows with thinned icing.

2. For Queen of hearts, position a marshmallow in center of heart cake and add tube 2 eyes and nose, tube 1 mouth, hair, necklace and eyebrows, tube 4 cheeks. Pipe crown with tube 3. Border heart cake with tube 3 inverted hearts, tube 2 dots.

3. For King of diamonds, pipe tube 48 ribbon on cake first, trim it with tube 1 string and set marshmallow on top. Pipe features the same as for queen. Add tube 2 hair, beard and mustache. Pipe tube 16 crown. Border diamond cake with tube 1 diamond pattern, centered with tube 1 dots. Edge with tube 3 beads.

4. For Jack of spades, mark space needed for Jack's head, then pipe tube 103 collar. Set marshmallow in place, and edge head and collar with tube 2 beads. Pipe features and hair same as for King and Queen. Add a tube 48 crown. Pipe spade trims with tube 2. On edge of cake, pipe tube 7 spades and tube 4 border.

5. For Ace of clubs cake, pipe a large letter "A", using *Celebrate! IV* pattern, or make your own. Pipe with tube 2, add tube 1 trim. Pipe large tube 7 clubs and bottom bead border. Edge top club with tube 1 dots.

for a rollicking dance

After all the sets are called, bring out this square dance cake for a grand finale. The evening's best dancers cut this colorful cake.

1. In advance, pipe tube 225 drop flowers. Add centers with tube 2. Make strands of hay with tube 3. Pipe pieces 2″ to 3″ long on waxed paper and let dry.

To make dancers and fiddle, tape *Celebrate! IV* patterns on stiff board, cover with waxed paper, outline with tube 1 and brown icing and flow in thinned icing. Pipe bow for fiddle over piece of florists' wire. Dry thoroughly, then add details with tube 1 and ruffles on skirts with tube 101s. Dry all pieces again.

2. Bake 8″ and 12″ two-layer square tiers. Fill and ice smoothly. Assemble on foil-covered board.

Pipe tube 8 bulbs around base of 12″ tier. Divide each side into sixths and pipe tube 104 ribbon swags around tier. Add tube 2 lettering on side, then pipe tube 8 bulbs around tier top. On 8″ tier, pipe tube 6 bulbs around base. Divide each side into fourths and pipe tube 104 ribbon swags around tier. Pipe tube 6 bulbs around top of tier.

3. Pipe mound of icing on top of cake and insert icing hay. Prop fiddle against mound, attaching with icing. Add drop flowers and pull out smaller pieces of hay with tube 3. On sides of tiers near back, pipe mounds of icing and attach drop flowers. Pull out pieces of hay with tube 3.

Attach dancers to front of tiers on mounds of icing. Serves 48.

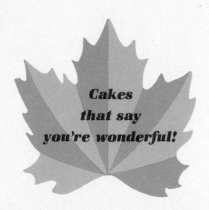

Cakes that say you're wonderful!

HERE ARE CAKES to honor small or large achievements in the life of someone you love. They look very impressive, but they're quick to do.

Congratulations!

A trophy filled with golden sunflowers is a tribute to a friend at retirement from business, a husband who earned a promotion, or a student who won that coveted degree. The trophy will be a lasting keepsake.

1. Make two dozen sunflowers of royal icing, using tube 124 for petals, tube 5 for centers and brown-tinted sugar for glitter. (Use daisy technique.) Mount twelve flowers on 4″ florists' wire stems. Pipe tube 67 leaves directly on wire stems. Paint a Classic Vase with thinned icing, mound stiffened icing in vase and arrange bouquet of wired flowers and leaves.

2. Bake, fill and ice an 11″ x 15″ x 4″ sheet cake and a 6″ x 2″ round tier. Assemble, setting the round tier back toward corner of the sheet cake. Write tube 4 message.

3. Edge sheet cake base with tube 22 commas. Divide long sides of cake into sixths, shorter sides into fourths, and pipe tube 18 star-and-shell design over each mark. Edge cake top with tube 18 swags, draped between star-and-shell designs. Overpipe swags with same tube for a full effect. Edge round cake base with tube 18 stars. Trim top edge with trios of tube 22 upright shells and pipe a single inverted tube 22 shell beneath each trio. Add a single tube 18 star where shell tips join.

Mound icing at each corner of sheet cake and push in sunflowers. Trim with tube 67 leaves. Position trophy on cake. Serves a party of 40.

You're our top banana!

For the star of the class show, the winner of top grades, or a favorite boss. This Quick & Pretty cake will bring an instant smile.

1. Model marzipan banana. (Recipe, page 23). A real banana is your best guide. Shape a piece of marzipan 6½″ long between your palms, taper at ends for typical banana shape. Paint brown flecks with food color thinned with a drop or two of kirsch. Dry, then brush with syrup glaze. (Bring one cup water, ½ cup corn syrup to a boil.) Add tube 1 eyes and pert smile.

2. Bake, fill and ice a two-layer oval cake. Edge base with tube 5 beading. Pipe a single row of tube 8 string drapes over beading and trim with tube 3 swirls. Pipe two rows of tube 3 string drapes just above first row and trim with swirls. Edge top of cake with tube 4.

Position banana on cake top and write tube 2 message. Crown banana with Candlelit Crown. Serves 12.

Coming up roses!

Are they retiring to a sunny spot? Celebrating an anniversary? Announcing wedding plans? Give them your best wishes with this blooming cake. Heap it with roses you've made ahead and stored.

1. Make lots of roses and rosebuds with tube 104 well ahead of time. If made of buttercream, store in the freezer until just before serving.

2. Bake a sheet cake, 9″ x 13″ x 4″. Fill and ice smoothly. Measure space needed for message and curve it across cake, using tube 2. Edge cake top with tube 16 shells.

3. Pipe tube 5 stems at one corner of cake, pulling them down on sides of cake. Pipe more stems at opposite corner of cake top. Set roses on mounds of icing. Add tube 66 leaves. Border cake base with tube 32 shells. Serves 24 guests.

Quick & Pretty

Quick & Pretty

Quick & Pretty

WOULDN'T IT BE FUN to have a party with a game theme? You can play the game before serving a cake that is a replica of the game board.

Backgammon is all the rage

1. Make marzipan (recipe, page 23). Tint small portions red and light brown, a larger portion dark brown. Roll out 1/16" thick and cut 15 red and 15 light brown disks with tube 2A. Cut twelve dark brown and twelve untinted triangles, 3" long and 1" wide at base. Model two red and three untinted cubes for dice. Dry, then brush pieces with syrup glaze (mix ½ cup corn syrup, 1 cup water and bring to boil).

2. Bake a 9" × 13" two-layer cake. Place on foil-covered board. Fill and ice smoothly. Pipe tube 16 shells around base of cake. Divide top exactly in half with a tube 3 string, then overpipe twice.

3. Pipe zigzag border on top of cake with tube 16. Attach triangles to cake top, ½" in from edges. Secure disks to triangles with icing. Pipe dots and numbers on cubes and set on cake top. Serves 24.

Old-fashioned Chinese checkers

1. Mold marzipan marbles in six colors (recipe, page 23). Dry, then brush with syrup glaze.

2. Bake cake in Hexagon Ring Pan. Ice smoothly. Set on tray or cake board. Pipe tube 17 bottom star border. Mark a six-sided star on top with edge of a piece of cardboard (make a line connecting every second corner). Pipe over marks and around center hole with tube 2.

3. Pipe dots in each section with tube 5 to represent the indentations for the marbles. Then fill areas with tube 13 stars, making the triangular ones the same colors as the marbles. Place a large candle in center hole. Serves twelve.

A game of chess

MAKE CHESSMEN

1. Make two recipes of marzipan as directed on page 23. Divide into four parts, tinting one red, one green, one brown and leaving one untinted. Take a small piece from untinted part and tint it gold. Roll out brown

Continued on page 134

129

ANNIVERSARY CAKES celebrate love's maturity, so they deserve all the skill and care you'd give in decorating a wedding cake.

See page 134 for a list of appropriate anniversary gifts.

Flowers and fruit for the fourth

Both adorn this cake with four candles to light the many years ahead.

1. In advance, make marzipan fruit in variety, using recipe and directions on page 23. Dry for a day or two, then brush with syrup glaze. Pipe tube 225 drop flowers.

2. Bake, fill and ice a two-layer 10″ square cake. Measure 1″ down from top and pipe triple tube 2 strings on three sides. Write couple's names on top, and message on plain side with tube 2. Pipe tube 8 bottom bulb border, tube 6 top border.

3. Mark a semi-circle on cake top with a toothpick. Pipe a thick tube 6 line on mark and set in fruits. Attach flowers with icing. Pipe front corner mounds and press in more fruit and flowers. Trim all with tube 67 leaves. Add candles. Serves 20.

A family tree

Decorate this cake for the happy couple blessed with grandchildren.

1. Cut enough round cookies for the portraits and one for the anniversary year with 1⅜″ round cutter. Also cut a 1″ heart cookie and a dog from the Animal Cutter set. Use recipe on page 147 or your own. Bake, outline with tube 1 and royal icing and fill in with thinned icing. Add the details with tube 1. Pipe anniversary year on one round cookie and edge it and small heart cookie with tube 2 beading.

2. Bake and fill a two-layer 9″ x 13″ sheet cake. Ice sides chocolate, top light blue. Pipe tube 15 tree trunk and branches. Pipe tube 1 "grass." Plan position of portraits. Pipe a cluster of tube 66 leaves and place cookie portraits. Finish with leaves.

3. Center heart cookie on long side of cake and pipe couple's names on either side of it with tube 2. Attach number cookie to shorter side of cake

and pipe tube 2 message. Edge cake base with tube 22 shells, top with tube 17 shells. Serves 24 guests.

Crystal for the 15th

Celebrate the occasion with a cake trimmed in glittering hard candy.*

1. Bake, fill and ice a 12″ x 4″ square tier and a 6″ x 3″ round tier. Assemble with Crystal Clear pillars and 8″ separator plate.

2. Divide sides of square tier into fourths and mark 2″ from bottom. Drop tube 2 strings from mark to mark. Pipe a tube 9 ball border at base, a tube 7 ball border at top. Using string curves on sides as guide, pipe tube 2 scallops on top.

3. Divide side of top tier into eighths. Mark 1¼″ down from top edge. Drop a tube 2 string from these marks and another just below it. Pipe tube 6 base border, tube 5 top border. Circle scallops around tier top with tube 2. Now pipe tube 2 dots with clear piping gel on the scallops on both tiers.

4. Mold the hard candy trims using recipe and directions on page 9. Mold ten hearts and 16 designs for base tier in Heart and Stars & Shapes candy molds. Mold two large hearts in Heart Cupcake pan. Using cupcake pan as guide, form stiff cloth-covered florists' wire into a heart shape, twisting ends of wire into a stem. Lay wire on one large heart, pour a little hot candy over it and attach second heart. Cool, insert stem in top tier. Write names of couple on heart with tube 1 and piping gel. Edge with gel beading.

Attach 3″ lengths of florists' wire to backs of two small hearts with hot candy. Cool, then insert in front of lower tier. Attach hard candy designs and hearts to tier sides with icing. Add candles. Serves 26.

*Do not attempt to mold hard candy in warm humid weather.

Sugar candy for the sixth

1. In advance, make sugar mold roses, leaves, bells and hearts.

2. Bake, fill and ice a two-layer 9″ x 13″ sheet cake. Pipe tube 17 shells at base and top, tube 17 scrolls at sides.

3. Print tube 3 message on cake top and pipe tube 3 bow above it. Attach sugar hearts and leaves in a large garland around message. Attach sugar bells beneath bow.

Attach small heart-and-leaf garlands on short sides of cake. Center sugar hearts on long sides. Write couple's name with tube 3. Serves 24.

Quick & Pretty

A masterpiece cake
decorated in the
dainty Australian manner

CREATE AN AUSTRALIAN CAKE for a very special anniversary or intimate wedding. Exquisitely decorated, but not as difficult as it might seem, this cake requires a steady hand for piping the delicate curtaining. Results are breathtaking!

Fashion the flowers

1. Make gum paste as directed on page 22. To make bluebells, roll out a small piece 1/16″ thick and cut flower with Flower Garden violet cutter. Flatten slightly, then elongate pet-als by pressing with modeling stick 3. Place on foam sponge and press in center with modeling stick 2 to form a cup shape. Make a tiny hole in center of flower, insert a pearl-tipped stamen and dry upside down. Wrap stem with floral tape. You need about seven bluebells.

2. To hand-model roses, model a cone from a ¾″ ball of gum paste. Flatten a ⅜″ ball into petal, thicker at one edge. Roll petal starting at thin edge and attach to top of cone with egg white. Make three more petals and attach around cone. Make five petals from a slightly larger ball. Cup pet-als and attach to cone. Furl edges. Make seven larger petals from a ½″ ball and attach to cone. Furl edges. Model a calyx on a piece of florists' wire and attach rose with egg white. Dry. You will need three roses.

3. Cut gum paste leaves using Flower Garden violet leaf cutter. Press into leaf mold and attach a piece of florists' wire to back with egg white. Dry. Tape flowers and leaves into a spray.

4. Cut three 4″ squares of fine nylon net. Attach to a piece of wax paper and pipe tube 1s scallops around edges, dots in middle. Dry. Pull each together in the center and secure with florists' wire. Tape spray of flowers, net handkerchiefs and a ribbon bow together into bouquet.

Covering the cake

1. Bake an 8″ x 3″ square fruitcake (a good recipe is on page 29, or use your own favorite). Make a recipe of marzipan (page 23) and roll it out about ⅜″ thick and large enough to cover cake. Brush cake with hot apricot glaze (heat one cup apricot jam to boiling and strain). Place marzipan over cake and press in place. Smooth with hands and trim excess.

2. Make a recipe of rolled fondant (see below). Roll out ¼″ thick and large enough to cover cake. Brush marzipan coating with apricot glaze and place fondant over cake. Smooth and trim excess. Smooth again and trim bottom edge perfectly even. Transfer cake to 13″ square, double-thick cake board.

ROLLED FONDANT

    2 pounds confectioners' sugar,
       sieved three times
    ½ ounce gelatin
    ¼ cup water
    ½ cup glucose
    ¾ ounce glycerine
    2 or 3 drops clear flavoring

1. Put gelatin and water in a small pan and heat gently until just dissolved. Put sieved sugar in a large bowl and make a well in center. Add glucose and glycerine to dissolved gelatin and mix well. Pour mixture into well in sugar and mix with your hands to a dough-like consistency.

2. Transfer to smooth surface lightly dusted with cornstarch and knead until smooth and pliable. Add flavoring while kneading. If too soft, knead in sieved sugar. If too stiff, add a few drops of boiling water.

3. Use immediately or store in an airtight container at room temperature for up to a week. Knead again before rolling out. If storing longer, refrigerate and bring to room temperature before kneading and rolling out. Recipe will cover an 8″ x 3″ square or 9″ x 3″ round cake.

Decorate the cake

1. Pipe tube 5 beading around base of cake. Measure circumference of cake with a 1″ strip of paper, fold into 20 divisions and make pattern for scallops. Mark scallops very accurately on sides of cake with tiny pin holes.

2. Pipe extension work. Drop a tube 2 string of royal icing along marked scallop and over-pipe four times, letting each line dry before piping another one. Position each line along outer edge of line beneath it to give the extension work an outward slant. When dry, paint the extension work with thinned royal icing. Dry.

3. Make curtaining. Pipe tube 1s strings from pin holes to extension work. To keep lines straight, pipe those at points of scallops first, then one directly in center. Divide the space on either side of center with a line and keep dividing open spaces until the scallop is covered with strings. Repeat around the cake. Pipe tube 1s beading along edge of extension work, then drop tiny string loops from it. Pipe tiny scallops along top of curtaining with tube 1s. Add dot flowers and leaves.

4. Attach pieces of ⅜″ wide ribbon to top of cake with tiny dots of icing at ends. With tube 1s, pipe dot flowers, leaves and beading along edges of ribbon. Make four tiny ribbon bows and attach with dots of icing where ribbons meet. Secure bouquet to top of cake with icing. Cut into 1″ x 2″ pieces. Serves 32.

The major foreign methods of cake decorating

The foreign methods are well worth studying and practicing. Their attractive techniques will add new charm to your own cakes—and they'll also give you a deeper understanding of the Wilton-American method. Here are capsule descriptions of the major foreign methods. Each is distinct and unmistakable.

THE PHILIPPINE METHOD. Masses of pastel flowers, delicately piped in unusual and speedy ways, are the hallmark of this method. Construction of cakes is ingenious and borders and trim are heavily piped.

THE ENGLISH METHOD. The highly developed art form in England has evolved into two distinct styles. *The Nirvana style* is characterized by architectural cakes covered with "run-in" work. *The Over-piped style* features impressive cakes notable for scrolls and borders piped and over-piped many times.

THE AUSTRALIAN METHOD produces dainty, perfectly proportioned cakes trimmed with lace, delicate veil-like curtaining and embroidery. Piped and modeled flowers are accents.

THE SOUTH AFRICAN METHOD is flamboyant and colorful. There are two styles within this method. *The Lacework style* features showy lace wings. *The Run-in style* is similar to the English Nirvana style, but the run-in frames enclose colorful, three-dimensional pictures.

THE MEXICAN METHOD is theatrical. Carefully dressed gum paste dolls are posed in realistic settings on large cakes that serve as stages. Pastillage is used to create buildings and platforms.

THE CONTINENTAL METHOD was originated and enlarged by European chefs. This method features the finest of baking with the exterior of the confection garnished and decorated to reflect and enhance the sweet within. Fine line piping, marzipan and molded and piped chocolate are frequently used.

WOULD YOU LIKE TO KNOW MORE about foreign method decorating? *The Wilton Way of Cake Decorating, Volume Two* devotes a full colorful chapter to each method. Close-up pictures display all details, then masterpiece cakes are shown and fully explained.

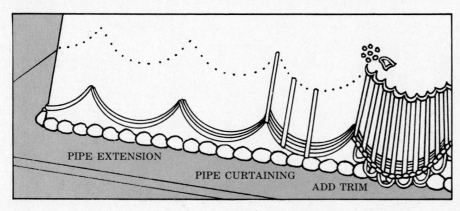

PIPE EXTENSION

PIPE CURTAINING

ADD TRIM

How to bake a Mallard duck

Shown on page 119

Bake this showpiece cake for a hunter, outdoorsman or nature-lover. It's challenging, but an exciting cake to create.

1. Make about ten gum paste cattails. (Recipe page 22.) Mold cylinders of brown gum paste around lengths of florists' wire. Roll out green gum paste and make many long slender leaves by cutting with a pastry cutter. Dry on a curve.

2. Make the duck from two layers of a 9″ × 13″ firm pound cake. *Celebrate! IV* patterns give complete diagrams to follow. Chill, then carve duck body with a sharp knife. Cut a cardboard cake board into a 7″ × 12″ oval and attach body to it with icing. Model duck's head from marzipan (recipe, page 23) following diagram. Make indentations for eyes. Insert a dowel rod part way into base of head for stability, then insert other end into body. Smooth head to body with icing. Ice head green, then add texture with brush. Cover beak with a thin piece of marzipan and press in details with a small rounded stick. Fill eye indentations with piping gel.

3. Smoothly ice underside of tail green. Ice breast with dark brown icing, giving feather effect by pulling icing away from cake with spatula. Ice rest of body with lighter brown, then pat with a clean, damp sponge to create a second feather effect. Pipe tube 44 ring around neck and a line at edge of underside of tail. Pipe tube 44 white "feathers" on tail, then add tube 80 green "feathers". Pipe wings in two shades of brown using tube 70. Smooth last row of "feathers" onto body with a damp brush. Add wing color with tube 2.

4. Bake a 12″ × 18″ × 3″ cake for base and swirl with boiled icing for water effect. Pipe tube 17 bottom shell border. Place mallard duck in center of cake. Attach cattails and leaves with icing to cake and board. Duck will serve 15 and base cake serves 54.

DRUM SET *continued*

white. Smooth seam and place on cardboard form to dry.

3. Pipe drum sticks on wax paper about 5½″ long using tube 10 and royal icing. Dry. Cut 1″ off plastic Mini-Tier pillars for legs to support small drums.

4. Bake a 10″ round two-layer cake and two 5″ two-layer round Mini-Tier cakes. Fill 10″ cake and insert four ¼″ dowel rods down into cake and clip off level with top. Ice top and sides of cake smoothly and sprinkle sides with edible glitter. Pipe lettering on top of cake.

To stand upright, place base against side of cake. Insert a spatula under cake and turn cake and base to an upright position carefully. Ice back of cake (this was the bottom) smoothly. Pipe tube 14 stars around edges of cake, then add tube 4 strings across the side of the cake. Push a 15″ long dowel rod down through cake and base, positioning it off to one side. Paint exposed portion of dowel with royal icing and secure cymbal to dowel with icing.

5. Assemble 5½″ separator plates from the round Mini-Tier set with the shortened pillars. Ice the 5″ cakes and set them on the plates. Sprinkle sides with edible glitter. Pipe tube 14 stars on edges and add tube 4 strings on sides as for bass drum. Set drum sticks on top and get ready for the party. Serves about 20.

A GAME OF CHESS *continued*

marzipan about ¹/₁₆″ thick and cut twelve triangles, 3″ wide at base and 2″ high. Also cut 32 1½″ brown squares. Dry, then brush the pieces with syrup glaze.

2. Roll out marzipan about ⅛″ thick and cut disks with wide end of tube 115 from red, green, brown and untinted. Assemble them for the bases of the figures, attaching with egg white. Use picture as a guide. For each of the opposing sets of figures make eight pawns, two rooks, two bishops, two knights, one queen and one king. Make ⅞″ diameter balls for the heads of the pawns, bishops, queens and kings. Cut disks for necks with narrow end of tube 12. Attach heads to necks with egg white. Model cone-shaped tops for rooks. Model helmet tops for knights by making rounded tops and plumes, then attaching with egg white. Dry all the pieces.

3. Cut 3″ × ¾″ pieces of marzipan for jerkins for the pawns. Attach to the bases with egg white, then cut a hole for the neck in the top of the jerkin with tube 12. Attach the heads to the bases of the pawns, bishops, queens and kings with icing. Cut tiny triangular pieces from gold marzipan.

Use them to create the six-pointed crowns for the queens and kings and the miters for the bishops. Attach with egg white. Secure the tops to the rooks and knights with icing. Dry, then brush all the figures with syrup glaze.

4. Trim the figures with tube 1 details. Make flags for rooks from colored paper. Cut triangles and attach to a straight pin with a line of icing. Pipe a dot of icing over the head of the pin. Dry, then pipe tube 1 heart on flag. Insert pin into point of cone.

DECORATE THE CAKE

Bake a 12″ × 4″ square cake. Place on cake board. Ice the top of the cake with a regular thickness of icing, but ice the sides with a very thin coat. Attach the marzipan squares to the top of the cake with dots of icing and the triangles to the base. Pipe tube 16 stars to cover the rest of each side. Attach the chess pieces to the top of the cake and set them around the base, using whatever game strategy you wish. Serves 36.

A guide for anniversary gifts

1st, *paper*	14th, *ivory*
2nd, *cotton*	15th, *crystal*
3rd, *leather*	20th, *china*
4th, *fruit, flowers*	25th, *silver*
5th, *wooden*	30th, *pearl*
6th, *sugar, candy*	35th, *coral*
7th, *woolen, copper*	40th, *ruby*
8th, *bronze, pottery*	45th, *sapphire*
9th, *willow, pottery*	50th, *golden*
10th, *tin, aluminum*	55th, *emerald*
11th, *steel*	60th, *diamond*
12th, *silk, linen*	75th, *diamond*

Celebrate!

Celebrate!®

NOVEMBER/DECEMBER...a time for sharing love

A Christmas ornament cake.
Directions on page 147

Quick & Pretty

136

IN THE MAD, GLAD rush before Christmas there's not much time to decorate—but you can still brighten the holiday table with handsome cakes like these that take only a little while to do.

Quick & Pretty

The bright bird of happiness

A cookie cutter serves as a pattern press to define the brilliant bird that sings on top of the cake.

1. Bake a two-layer 8″ square cake, fill and ice smoothly. Press giant Flying Bird cutter on top of cake to form design. Outline shape with tube 2, defining wing and tail areas. Fill in wings with tube 68 leaves, starting at tip. Do the tail the same way. Fill in rest of bird with tube 14 stars. Over-pipe eye.

2. Mark a curved line on top and each side of cake with a toothpick as guide for garlands. Pipe tube 68 leaves on either side of line. Add a red bow piped with tube 104 on side garlands. Finish with tube 17 shell borders. Serves twelve happy guests.

Pipe a patchwork wreath

Bright Christmas colors and quaint calico design make this cake a cheery holiday showpiece.

1. Bake your favorite cake recipe in the Party Ring Mold. Ice smoothly and pipe tube 15 star base border on inner ring. Divide outer edge of top into eight sections. On inner edge of top, mark center of each section. Connect points with a toothpick to form triangles on curved top of cake. Fill in triangles with tube 15 stars, alternating red and green. Fill in areas on cake side, below triangles, with stars.

2. Make calico print on open areas with tube 15 red stars. Trim each with a tube 65s leaf. Finish with a smashing red satin bow. Serves 20.

Sing out joy!

Measure your decorating time in minutes when you trim this beautiful little cake!

1. Bake a two-layer cake in 8″ pans. Fill, then ice smoothly. Pipe "Joy" with tube 14 and do bottom shell border with tube 19.

2. Mark a 6″ circle on top of cake with a toothpick. Pipe tube 70 leaves on either side of circle. Set candied cherries on wreath. Pipe a group of five leaves at four points on base of cake. Trim with cherries. Serve to twelve merry-makers.

A shining candelabra cake

Use tube 18 and tinted icing to turn out this handsome holiday cake!

1. Bake and ice a 9″ × 13″ × 3″ cake. Pipe a puffy fleur-de-lis on each corner at base. Now pipe six fleurs-de-lis on long side of base, and four on shorter side to form side trim. Add an edging of stars.

2. Pipe candelabra. Make a mark in the center and 3″ from front edge of cake. Pipe a long "C" on either side of mark for outer arms of candelabra. Trim with curved shells.

Pipe two more "C's" within these for inner arms, then two short ones in center. Top each "C" with a swirl for candle holder.

Pipe candelabra base with a fleur-de-lis and two "S" curves. Top with a star. Pipe candles and flames with short strokes and add shell border at top of cake. Serves 24.

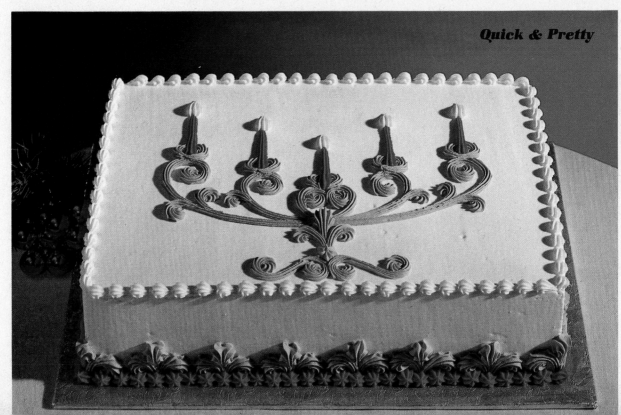

Quick & Pretty

Quick
&
Pretty

Christmas garland *upper left*

Bake a 10″ × 4″ round cake. Ice and place on serving tray. Mark overlapping designs on sides with a Pattern Press and pipe with tube 16. Pipe tube 19 bottom and tube 17 top shell borders, adding a tube 15 star between each shell. Set candle on top of cake and circle with tube 17 shells. Serves 14.

Parade of elves *lower left*

1. Bake Long Loaf cake and four small Wonder Molds. Ice Long Loaf and place on serving tray. Cut Wonder Molds in half, ice and attach to cake with icing.

2. Pipe tube 112 holly leaves on wax paper, pulling out points with a damp brush. Dry or freeze.

3. Pipe a 1″ high tube 16 zigzag around base of cake and Wonder Molds. Pipe tube 103 ruffle around tops of Wonder Molds. For elf heads, cut four marshmallows in half, paint with thinned icing, and attach to side of cake. Pipe arms with tube 2A, faces with tube 1. Tie small candy canes with ribbons and attach to arms with icing.

4. Pipe tube 16 top shell border. Pipe a tube 4B star on top of each marshmallow and add a tube 4 ball.

5. Insert four tapers into cake top. Attach holly leaves with icing around tapers and on ends of cake, then pipe tube 4 berries. Long Loaf serves 16, each elf serves one.

Bright little treats *upper right*

MAKE DRUMS. Bake cakes in 10¾ ounce condensed soup cans, chill and cut each in half. Ice, then pipe tube 47 zigzag around edges. Add tube 3 strings and tube 15 stars. Cover toothpicks with icing for drumsticks and pipe tube 7 balls on ends.

CHRISTMAS TREE CUPCAKES. Cover ice cream cones with tube 74, pulling out points of icing. Pipe tube 16 star on top and attach red cinnamon candies with dots of icing. Bake cupcakes, ice and pipe a tube 124 ruffle around edge. Place a tree on each.

A curly Christmas tree *lower right*

Bake a cake in a decorative pan about 9″ × 13″. Leave cake in pan, ice top and mark triangle to indicate tree shape. Starting at base, pipe tube 18 curls to fill in. Add candles and flames. Pipe tube 190 flower at top and center with tube 18 star. Serves about 24.

Continental Chocolates for the holidays

Chef Olkiewicz shares his fabulous recipes for European candies that you can make in your own kitchen. Be sure to temper all chocolate before using—instructions on page 44.

WIENERBONBONS
(Viennese Bonbons)

8 ounces almond paste
6 ounces sweet butter
1½ ounces confectioners' sugar
3 ounces cherry brandy
18 ounces tempered dark chocolate, reheated
3 ounces toasted ground hazelnuts
Whole toasted hazelnuts
2 pounds tempered dark chocolate
Milk chocolate for trim

1. Make bases for filling by rolling almond paste ⅛″ thick. Cut with a 1″ round cutter.
2. Beat butter and confectioners' sugar until fluffy. Add cherry brandy and beat again. Mix in reheated dark chocolate. Add ground hazelnuts and mix until it is a soft fudge-like consistency. Place mixture in parchment cone and drop out onto bases in spiral mound. Cool in refrigerator one hour.
3. Place a whole hazelnut on top and dip on a bent fork into tempered dark chocolate. Decorate with a spiral and star. Yields 80 to 100 candies.

PFLAUMENKUESSCHEN
(Prune Kiss)

80 small pitted prunes
Bourbon whiskey
8 ounces almond paste
2 to 4 ounces apricot brandy
2 pounds tempered dark chocolate
Milk chocolate for trim

1. Marinate prunes in bourbon in a covered jar for one week. Drain in a sieve, then dry on paper towels.
2. Mix almond paste with enough apricot brandy to form a soft paste. Fill prunes well with mixture. Refrigerate one hour. Dip into tempered dark chocolate on a bent fork and decorate with milk chocolate leaves and rosette. Makes 80 Prune Kisses.

NOUGATKROKANT

2 pounds tempered dark chocolate
1 pound 10 ounces nougat (purchase in import candy section of grocery)
5 ounces white vegetable shortening
9 ounces Krokant (recipe below)
3 ounces chopped candied orange peel
Milk chocolate for trim

1. Make chocolate cups in plastic Oval Candy Molds. Fill molds with tempered chocolate, then tip to empty excess. Place in refrigerator for ten minutes and remove from mold.
2. Beat nougat and shortening until fluffy. Add krokant and candied orange peel and mix well. Fill chocolate cups with mixture almost to the top. Pipe dark chocolate on top to seal, then pipe milk chocolate leaves on one edge. 80 to 100 candies.

KROKANT

6 ounces sugar
1 teaspoon glucose or corn syrup
3 ounces sliced, toasted almonds

Melt sugar to a dark brown color. Stir in glucose, remove from heat and add almonds. Pour onto a greased baking sheet to cool and harden, then roll with a rolling pin to break it up into very fine pieces.

Holly Cascade

Create this cake for a wedding, an anniversary or Christmas party.

1. Using Flower Garden cutter, make gum paste holly leaves (recipe, page 22) and berries on wires following instruction booklet. Tape into sprays.
2. Bake 6″, 10″ and 14″ round two-layer tiers. Fill, ice and assemble on a foil-covered board.
3. Pipe tube 17 double puffs around base of 14″ tier. Add tube 14 scallop above and below each. Pipe tube 14 fleurs-de-lis and tube 16 rosettes between puffs. Around top edge pipe tube 16 double puffs with tube 14 fleurs-de-lis and tube 16 rosettes between them. Pipe similar borders on 10″ tier with tube 14 and on 6″ tier with tube 13.
4. Remove cherub from Kneeling Cherub Fountain and place fountain upside down on top tier. Remove flat plates from push-in filigree pedestals and replace with Crystal Clear candle holders. Insert two pedestals in side of top tier, three each in middle and bottom tiers.
5. Attach holly sprays to top ornament and to pedestals for cascade. Insert candles. Serves 156 wedding-style or 46 party-style.

Holly Cascade
Decorating directions at left

Be creative with cookies

Fill your house with the wonderful aroma of cookies in the oven. It's the very perfume of Christmas! Bake all the traditional treats your family loves—but save a little time to make these new cookie creations, too. They'll charm everyone.

Riding home

This little cookie rider is hurrying home through the snowy dusk—perhaps to be on time to trim the tree. Create this poetic scene.

1. Use *Celebrate! IV* patterns to cut the cookie pieces. The horse is cut from gingerbread dough and the trees and rider from Roll-out cookie dough. (Recipes page 147.) Lay the two trees on popsicle sticks to bake, so extended sticks can be pushed into cake. Do the same for the horse's two legs that touch the ground. Reinforce the point where the horse's tail joins body by pressing a toothpick into dough. Bake and cool very thoroughly.

2. Assemble horse with royal icing as picture shows. Attach ear piece to head, then two legs to body. Dry, then turn over and do the same on the other side, using pattern as guide in positioning legs.

Assemble rider. Attach cuff of hat, scarf, arm and leg to one side of body. Dry, then attach to horse with dots of icing where rider's leg and body touches. Dry again, then turn horse and rider over and attach remaining parts of rider. Make a little bridle from gold cord and secure ends in rider's hands.

3. Bake a 9″ x 13″ x 3″ cake. Set on cake board and swirl on icing. Dust with edible glitter. Pipe tube 16 base border. Push trees into cake, then carefully push in horse and rider. Serves 24.

A cookie cottage

In lots of homes, Christmas wouldn't be Christmas without a gingerbread house. Here's a new-style one with a quaint mansard roof.

1. Use the gingerbread recipe on page 147, or your own. Use Roll-out recipe for the door. Roll out and cut parts, using *Celebrate! IV* patterns. Also cut a 11″ x 11″ base for the house and a 1½″ x 3″ piece for message. Bake, then cool completely.

2. Use tube 2 and royal icing to outline open areas and add trim to sides of house and door. Be creative—this is Christmas! Tint gum paste in bright colors (page 22), roll out and cut many circles using end of standard tube. These will be "shingles" for roof. Cut circles with end of any large tube for path. Dry.

3. Assemble the house with royal icing. Mark a 5″ x 6½″ rectangle on base cookie to indicate position of house. Attach base cookie to 14″ x 14″

Continued on page 147

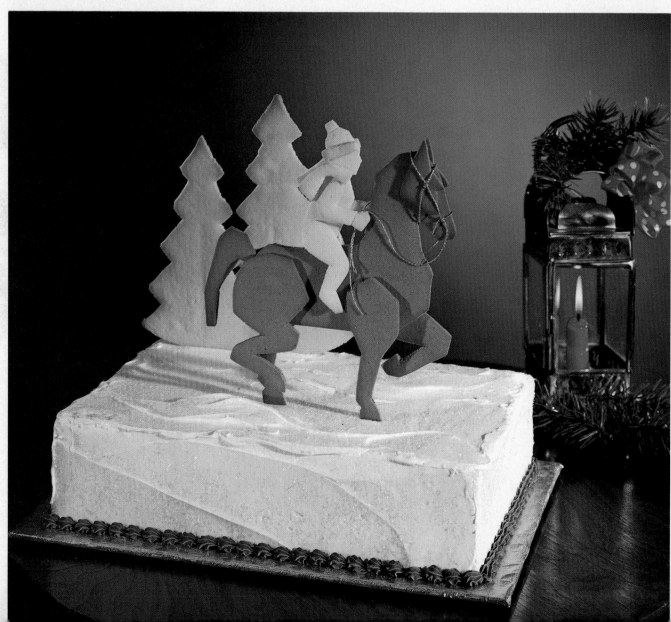

Cookie treats
for the
holidays

Santah and his elves frolic on a jolly cake in the Nirvana style

THE ENGLISH NIRVANA STYLE, with its panels of run-in work is a perfect technique for this colorful cake with a Christmas theme.

The typical English cake is a firm, moist fruitcake (recipe on page 29) that is covered with a smooth layer of marzipan and then iced with two thin coats of royal icing.

Do the run-in work

Although the English use egg-white royal icing for their run-in work, we use Color Flow because it is easier to work with and dries faster. Use recipe on Color Flow mix can. To thin it for running in, put some icing into a container and add a few drops of water at a time, stirring by hand. To test for proper consistency, spoon out a teaspoon of icing and let it drop back into container. When spoonful disappears to a count of ten, icing is the right consistency. After thinning, let icing sit, covered, 24 hours for air bubbles to surface.

Using *Celebrate! IV* patterns, tape collar and splay patterns flat to pieces of glass or plexiglas. Tape elf patterns to a 10″ curved surface. Cover smoothly with wax paper or plastic wrap. Using icing straight from batch, outline collars and splays with tube 2, elves and Santa with tube 1s. Dry, then begin to run-in icing, making sure you have

two bags filled and ready when running-in collars and splays.

The order of running-in the pieces is very important to keep a smooth finish on the work. Color Flow crusts quickly and crust lines will show on finished piece. For the collars and splays, follow the order on the diagram. Work quickly so the icing blends. Try to keep pieces thin and flat.

When the run-in work is complete, dry the pieces under a heat lamp placed two feet above them for two hours. This will give a glossy finish. Then complete drying for 72 hours.

After pieces dry, pipe tube 2 beading around bottom collar, top collar, bottom splay and top splay. Dry.

Pipe tube 65 holly leaves on wax paper, pulling out points with a damp brush. Dry. Attach to top collar and top splay. Pipe tube 2 berries at base of leaves.

Trim figures with tube 1s. Pipe spots on horse with tube 2 and flatten with a damp finger. Paint names on buckets with small brush and food color. Pipe star at top of tree with tube 16 and flatten with damp finger.

Please turn the page

Preparing the cake

Bake three 8″ round fruitcakes 2″ high and stack them, filling with apricot glaze until 6¼″ high. Cover with marzipan (recipe on page 23). Attach an 8″ cake circle on top of cake with royal icing. Pack space between cardboard and cake and fill any holes with marzipan. This board is now bottom of cake.

Roll a ball of marzipan into a 10″ circle, ⅜″ thick. Brush cake top with apricot glaze (heat one cup apricot jam to boiling and strain). Place cake upside down on marzipan, then cut around it. Turn upright. Brush sides with apricot glaze.

Shape remaining marzipan into a narrow roll and roll flat. Trim one long side straight. Place cake side on strip, bottom edge along straight edge. Roll, patting marzipan into place. Trim seam so edges butt.

Turn cake upright and trim excess marzipan. Press seams together and smooth. Dry 48 hours, then ice smoothly with two coats of royal icing. For cake board, use a 16″ diameter masonite circle covered with foil.

Assembling the cake

1. Center bottom collar pattern on board and lightly draw around it with a pencil. Remove pattern and pipe tube 4 riser lines on board within pattern lines. Attach cake in center of board with dots of icing. Pipe tube 2 beads around base of cake. Pipe risers on bottom collar where indicated on pattern. Pipe two tube 3 lines on top of each other, then add one tube 2 line. Dry.

2. Pipe dots of icing between riser lines on board. Carefully slip bottom collar over cake and, matching with pattern drawn on board, set on riser lines. Pipe a tube 2 line on risers on bottom collar. Then, matching design with bottom collar, slip top collar over cake and place on risers. Divide cake side into sixths, center elves and attach with icing.

3. Pipe risers on bottom splay where shown on pattern. Pipe two tube 3 lines, then one tube 2 line. Dry. Pipe dots of icing on top of cake, then center bottom splay on cake. Pipe another tube 2 line on risers and center top splay on them, matching design with bottom splay.

4. To serve cake, break run-in panels by tapping with a silver knife. Then cut into 1″ x 2″ pieces, treating each 2″ high layer as a tier. Serves 90.

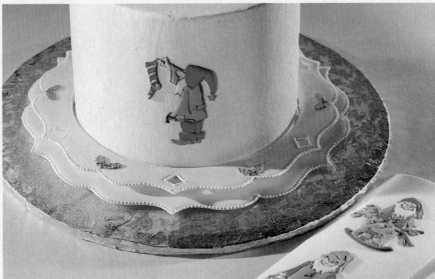

COOKIE COTTAGE *continued*

foil-covered board. Pipe tube 8 line on one side and back of marked rectangle and set one side wall in position on line. Pipe a line on side edge of side wall and set back wall on base. Prop with food cans while you add other two walls. Add entry in same way. Then dry thoroughly.

Remove cans and add roof. Pipe a tube 8 line of icing on top of one side wall and on top of back wall. Set one side of roof on wall, pipe line of icing on edge and position back of roof. Have a helper hold these two sections while you add other side and front of roof. Pipe line of icing all around roof and position top of roof. Add roof to entry. When roof is dry, assemble chimney on top of it. Dry thoroughly.

Lay whole tree on table and pipe a tube 8 line of icing down center. Set one half-tree on line and prop till dry. Set tree upright and pipe line of icing down center of other side. Position other half-tree on line and prop till thoroughly dry.

4. Pipe tube 16 rope on seams of house. Starting at base, cover roof of house with gum paste "shingles". Pipe "bricks" on chimney with tinted icing. Attach circles for path. Pipe tube 16 border around base. Thin boiled icing and swirl on house and base. Set tree on base and add icing to branches. Dust all lavishly with edible glitter. Set completed cottage in the place of honor in the living room. You may store the cottage, carefully covered, in a cool, dark place. Bring it out for several Christmases to come.

Cookie recipes

ROLL-OUT COOKIES
1¼ cups butter
2 cups sugar
2 eggs
5 cups flour
3½ teaspoons baking powder
1 teaspoon salt
½ cup milk
¼ teaspoon grated orange peel

A Christmas ornament *shown on page 135*

This fabulous cake will star as a beautiful centerpiece for a holiday party—or, if you're very generous, a magnificent gift. The ornament can be carefully lifted off before serving.

1. Make gum paste trims. (Recipe page 22). Mold an angel head with Baroque mold, following instructions that come with molds. Dry 48 hours, then paint with thinned royal icing. Dry thoroughly.

Make circles that serve as bases for filigree stars. Roll gum paste ¼" thick. With cookie cutters, cut a 3⅝" circle and two 1" circles. Roll tinted gum paste very thin and cut eight pink circles with large end of a standard tube and eight green circles with end of tube 1A.

2. Make Color Flow and filigree stars. Tape *Celebrate! IV* patterns to stiff board and cover smoothly with wax paper.

For large star, clip eight pieces of cloth-covered florists' wire to length of center line on filigree area. Cover with icing by inserting in decorating cone fitted with tube 2. Dry on wax paper, then lay in position on pattern. Outline center and eight petal-shaped areas with tube 2. Do filigree areas with tube 1. Flow in solid areas with thinned icing. Dry 48 hours, then overpipe solid areas with tube 2 and attach pink and green circles. Dry again.

For small star, pipe outline of center circle and main line of filigree petals with tube 2. Pipe filigree with tube 1. Flow in center circle with thinned icing. Dry 48 hours.

3. Assemble ornament with royal icing. Attach large, 8-pointed star to 3⅝" gum paste circle. Center with 1" circle, then attach small filigree star. Attach another 1" circle and secure angel.

4. Use the fruitcake recipe on page 29, or your own, to bake an 8" round cake, 3" high. Cover cake with apricot glaze. (Heat one cup apricot preserves to boiling and strain.)

Set cake on silver tray and wrap a 1" strip of wax paper around side. Wrap a 1" wide ribbon over strip, securing with dots of royal icing. Pin a fluffy bow to ribbon. Cut a 3⅝" diameter circle from wax paper and place in center of cake. Set ornament on circle. This never-before cake cuts into thirty 1" x 2" pieces.

Cream butter and sugar together, then add eggs and beat till fluffy. Sift dry ingredients together and add alternately to creamed mixture with milk. If mixture is too sticky, add enough flour to make it easy to handle. Roll dough ¼" thick and cut. Lift cookies with a large spatula and place on an ungreased cookie sheet. Bake in 375° oven for eight minutes.

GRANDMA'S GINGERBREAD
5 to 5½ cups all-purpose flour
1 teaspoon baking soda
1 teaspoon salt
2 teaspoons ginger
2 teaspoons cinnamon
1 teaspoon nutmeg
1 teaspoon cloves
1 cup shortening
1 cup sugar
1¼ cups unsulphured molasses
2 eggs, beaten

1. Thoroughly mix flour, soda, salt and spices.

2. Melt shortening in large saucepan. Add sugar, molasses and eggs, then mix well. Cool the mixture slightly, then add four cups dry ingredients and mix very well.

3. Turn mixture onto lightly-floured surface. Knead in remaining dry ingredients by hand. Roll dough to ⅛" thickness. Cut out pieces with cutter or knife. Place on greased cookie sheets with spatula. Roll large pieces on cookie sheet, cut out, and remove excess dough from edges.

4. Bake at 375°F for eight to ten minutes, depending on size. Let cool on cookie sheet a few minutes before removing to rack to cool completely.

A glittering Christmas cake in pulled sugar

Norman Wilton created this spectacular cake for the anniversary of a boutique, but it is just as appropriate for your own Christmas celebration. Just as with all techniques, practice is essential for pulled sugar.

Equipment you'll need

For making pulled sugar you'll need a six-quart heavy aluminum pan, a candy thermometer, a 2′ x 3′ marble slab, a sturdy metal scraper, an 18″ strip of heavy canvas about four feet long, two large strong tables, a wood-framed screen of fine 40- to 60-gauge copper mesh, an electric heater, scissors, clean pastry brush and food colors.

Getting ready

Before beginning, be sure to read through this section completely. The order of work is important. Start with pulling ribbons to cover the sides of the cake and with bows, while the sugar is most pliable. Flowers and other small trims are made last. Any sugar you are not working with should be kept on the screen in front of the heater. Turn it from time to time to keep it evenly warm and pliable.

PREPARE THE CAKE. Bake a 12″ two-layer round cake using a firm pound cake recipe. Coat with apricot glaze, then cover it with rolled fondant as described on page 133.

SET UP WORK AREA. Set the marble slab on a sturdy table. Clean the marble, dry, then grease it thoroughly with solid white vegetable shortening. Set up the heater with the guard removed and lay the copper screen in front of it. Stretch the canvas strip over the remaining area of the table. Have your other equipment conveniently at hand.

Pulled Sugar Recipe

10 cups granulated cane sugar
  (Beet sugar tends to boil over)
2½ cups water
1 teaspoon, slightly mounded,
  cream of tartar

Add water to sugar and mix by hand until mixture is smooth and all lumps have dissolved. Add cream of tartar and cook to 312°F, washing down the sides of the pan about ten times while cooking with a wet pastry brush to keep crystals from forming. The faster the sugar is cooked, the whiter the mixture. The recipe will take about 40 minutes to cook on a household range. Yield: five pounds—will decorate a 12″ cake.

How the experts do it: Norman Wilton

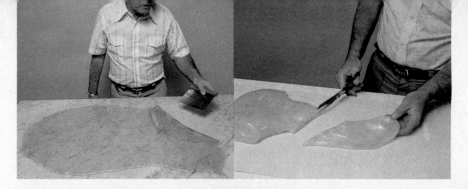

1. Pour the sugar on marble. Wait one minute, then start flipping the edges in to the center with the scraper. As you flip, the sugar will start to cool and stiffen. Keep working it until it forms a large ball.

2. Pulling the sugar. Cut off a piece and put remainder in front of heater. Begin to pull the piece. Lift one end and drop it over the other, then lift the other end and drop it in a pendulum motion, alternating hands. Pull until it is opaque. Place in front of heater to keep warm.

To tint a piece of sugar, place a little paste color on it before pulling. Stretch the sugar and fold it over the color, then pull as described above. For this cake, take one-fourth of the batch, divide this section in half and tint one piece red and one green. Also tint a very small piece yellow for poinsettia stamens.

3. Wrapping the cake. Cut off a piece of sugar about 11″ long, 2″ wide and 1″ thick. Stretch it out into a thin ribbon. Fold ribbon in half at an angle so it almost doubles in width. Run your hand over it to join the two lengths. Continue to stretch, smooth and fold until the ribbon is about 40″ long and 5″ wide. Work quickly. Cut off rough end of ribbon and quickly wrap around side of cake, tucking ends together to fasten. Gently touch top edges to ripple.

4. Make ruffle for base of cake. Pull out a long ribbon about 2″ wide x 24″. Ruffle by gently pinching between thumbs and forefingers. Attach with small pieces of sugar touched to heater, then base of cake. Continue until cake is completely edged.

5. Make striped ribbons. Lay a 6″ x 2″ green strip of sugar between two white strips the same size on the canvas, sides touching. Press pieces together with your hands. Pull out to twice its length, cut in half and place the two pieces side by side. Press to join, then pull out to about 1″ wide. Work very quickly. Cut into 8″ lengths and attach four ribbons around side of cake in curves. Attach the same as for the ruffle.

6. Make loops. Using striped ribbon as described above, cut into 4″ lengths, form into loops and set *on edge* to cool. You will need about five loops for each bow.

Cut off a 1½″ piece of candy and roll it with a rolling pin. Touch this plaque to heater, then to where two of the curved ribbons meet. Repeat for the

other three bows. Then attach loops by touching end to heat element and then to the plaque.

7. Make leaves. It is important to learn to make a leaf properly since almost all flower petals resemble leaves before assembling. Work in front of the heater to keep sugar soft.

Stretch a small piece of green sugar to thin it by pulling it out with both hands. Place your thumb in the sugar and pull it out to form the leaf. Squeeze between thumb and forefinger and twist to snap off or cut off. Press in leaf mold to vein.

8. Make roses. You will need three. Pull out two rounded petals just as for leaves. Curl one side of one petal, then place the other petal within it and roll so they are interlocked. Pull out three more petals and press around interlocked center of bud.

Pull out a petal, forming into a cup shape around your thumb and curl outer edges under. Make three more petals the same. Press each petal to the next as they are made to form a half-circle. Press the two outer petals together to form a cup shape. Cool completely, then touch base of bud to heater and insert into cup.

9. Make poinsettias. You will need two. Make six outer petals, each about 2½" x ⅝". Pull out a piece of sugar and snap it off. Stretch edges to ruffle and pinch tip into a point. Curve tip down and cool. Make five shorter petals about 2" long.

Roll a ½" ball for center. Attach outer petals first, touching base to heater, then to ball. Attach shorter petals the same way. Make stamens by pulling a piece of sugar into a fine strand. Cut into ¼" lengths. Pick up each with tweezers, touch to heater, then to center of flower.

10. Make scroll. Pull out a ribbon 3" wide and fold over to make thicker. Cut to 9" length. Roll two ends for scroll effect. Cool. Make small triangular pieces of sugar to support scroll. Attach to back of scroll by touching piece to heater, then to scroll. Place on top of cake.

11. Make twining vine. Pull out a round strand of sugar about the diameter of a pencil. Clip it off about three feet long. When cooled slightly, wrap it around a clean broomstick. Just before the sugar hardens and is still warm to the touch, pull the vine off the broomstick and shape it into a circle. Then place it on the cake.

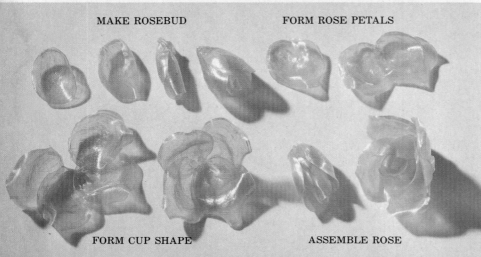

MAKE ROSEBUD   FORM ROSE PETALS

FORM CUP SHAPE   ASSEMBLE ROSE

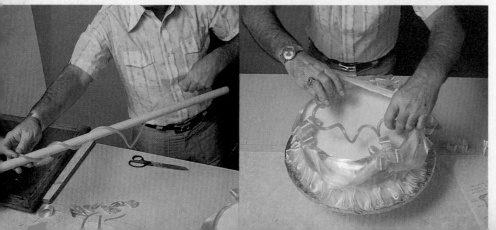

Indian corn for Thanksgiving

Create this autumn sheet cake adorned with ears of Indian corn to grace your Thanksgiving table. It's quite easy to do because the ears of corn are piped in buttercream icing directly on the cake.

1. Bake a 9″ x 13″ x 4″ sheet cake. Ice top beige, sides brown and place on a foil-covered board. With tube 10, pipe zigzags of buttercream icing on top of cake about 7″ long and 2″ wide for the ears of corn. Smooth the buttercream zigzags with a spatula, then mark lines as a guide for piping the rows of kernels with a toothpick.

2. Pipe kernels with tube 353 so they completely cover the ears. Then pipe leaves at top of ears with tube 115. Add a tube 104 bow.

3. Pipe tube 8 bottom ball border and tube 6 top ball border. Add tube 115 leaves at each corner. Serves 24.

off the broomstick and shape it into a circle. Then place it on the cake.

12. Finishing the cake. Attach a small piece of soft sugar to base of each flower. Touch this piece to the heater and fuse to vine. Add leaves by touching base to heater and immediately attaching to vine.

Make a Color Flow plaque using your own pattern, and trim it with tube 1 and royal icing. Attach to scroll with royal icing. Or you may pipe message directly on scroll.

Pull out a ¾″ wide red ribbon and ruffle it. Attach it over the lower part of the scroll and extending out over the sides. Your shining pulled sugar cake serves 22.

Norman

How color can give personality to a cake

The three identical cakes at left are an excellent picture lesson in the use of color in decorating.

The cake at top is sweetly feminine. The pink roses are complemented by the jade green plaque.

The middle cake uses a warm exciting scheme of yellow, moss green and brilliant scarlet.

The groom's cake at bottom is done in the simplest and most subtle scheme of all. Rich natural tones of chocolate set off the marzipan plaque. See how the texture on the cake sides gives an interesting play of light and shadow.

Experiment yourself with tinted icing. You'll enjoy seeing the effect of one color on another—and learn how color can turn the simplest cake into a work of art.

How to tint icing

Keep a good assortment of food colors on hand—it's much easier and quicker to use the colors right from the bottle or jar, rather than to blend two or more to the shade you want. The colors are cleaner too. An exception is flesh color. Add Pink to Copper. For sun tan, add Brown to Copper.

For a pastel tint, liquid food color is best. If you want a deeper hue, use paste color. Add very small amounts of either to white icing and mix well with a spatula. If color is too pale, add a bit more food color. Remember that buttercream deepens as it stands.

For natural looking flowers, I sometimes leave the icing a little "streaky". The varied tints make the petals very realistic.

Wilton...commonsense

Proven techniques of flower arrangement

I know that many of you have a keen interest in this aspect of decorating. While every flower arrangement is unique, there are a few general rules to follow to show off the flowers at their best.

Guidelines for a flower spray

A simple spray on a cake top is perhaps the most frequently used decoration. Start by observing the flowers in nature. Note that there are no straight lines—all flowers grow in graceful curves.

ALWAYS START WITH STEMS. The graceful curves of stems define the design and provide a structure for placing the flowers. Use your whole arm to pipe the stems and keep the decorating cone as close to flat on the cake surface as possible.

SET FLOWERS ON ICING MOUNDS. Never place a flower flat on the cake. First pipe a mound, then place the flower on it, tilting it so it appears at its best advantage.

KEEP LARGER FLOWERS AT BASE of spray, to give strength to the design. When you pipe the flowers, always vary them in size, and pipe a few buds, too. Then position the larger, heavier flowers at the base, moving out to the buds.

A spray of roses on a brithday cake

The pictures show how the spray develops. Notice how even the stems make an attractive design. A few leaves and ferns are added, then the flowers are put on. Three large full-bloom roses are set on the base of the spray, then smaller roses and finally buds at the end of the spray. Frame with more leaves.

Since I wanted a subtle color scheme, I striped the cone with brown before filling it with moss-green icing for the stems and leaves. The roses are in varying tints of pink. I prefer royal icing for flowers—you can make and store them in advance and they handle much more easily than buttercream flowers. Guests like them as souvenirs, too.

The script message is shown in the last picture so that you can see how the spray was made, but normally it would be piped first.

A graceful double spray

The double spray is another traditional flower design that gives the decorator a lot of opportunity for interesting effects. Here we used daisies and bluebells for a nice contrast in form and color. Pipe royal icing flowers in advance.

Pipe the stem arrangement just as you did for the rose spray on page 153, but pipe two groups of stems that meet in the center in an arch.

Mass the flowers in the center of the arch. Place the daisies on mounds of icing, tilting them forward and to either side. Then add bluebells in the same way until the arrangement is full and fluffy. Taper the flowers on either side, allowing more space between them as you near the ends of the stems. Then frame with leaves.

DECORATE THE CAKE. The cake is a two-layer 10″ round, iced in yellow to set off the flowers. Pipe a star border at base with tube 19 and drape it with tube 3 string. After the spray is put on the cake, drop double tube 3 strings on the side, then pipe a tube 363 shell top border. Pipe a "C" scroll around each shell and add a tube 66 leaf at points of string drape.

A six-part cascade

The classic cascade offers a way to bring flowers from the top of a cake down the sides for a soft, rounded effect. When the clusters are placed in a symmetrical arrangement, as on this cake, the design is very pleasing. Pipe the sweet peas in advance in royal icing.

DECORATE THE CAKE before adding flowers. This cake is a 10″ two-layer round. Pipe tube 16 star border at base and drape with tube 3 string. Divide top of cake into sixths and leave a 1″ space between each division. Pipe curved garlands on side of cake with tube 5, then pipe scallop on top with same tube. Drop a double tube 3 string over garlands. Edge top of cake with tube 16 reverse shells. Pipe tube 2 name in center of cake.

ARRANGE THE FLOWER CASCADES. Pipe stems and leaves on cake sides between garlands to define the shape of cascades. Now add the sweet peas on mounds of icing, working from edge of cake toward center, then down side. Notice that the sweet peas are in varied tints of pink.

An asymmetrical cascade

A large cascade that drapes from cake top to cake board is a very dramatic trim. Larger flowers are used in this cascade, with small blossoms to fill in. We piped lilies, wild roses and forget-me-nots in advance in royal icing.

FIRST DECORATE THE CAKE. Ice a two-layer 10″ round cake. At even intervals, pipe twelve upright shells from base to top with tube 22. Fill in base with tube 32 stars. Pipe a tube 347 scallop border on top of cake, then top each column with a tube 347 rosette.

DO THE CASCADE. Pipe a series of curved stems on the cake top in a shallow "C" shape. Pipe stems on side of cake to continue curve. Add leaves piped with tube 66. Now add the flowers on mounds of icing. Tilt them so they appear at best advantage. Mass them on the top of cake, near the edge, and taper off on either side. First place the largest flowers, the lilies, then the wild roses. Fill in with the forget-me-nots and complete with a few more leaves.

A double cascade of roses frames a tier cake

This splendid cake is suitable for a golden anniversary, or for a wedding. The feature is the double cascade of beautiful roses and buds in shades of yellow. Cascades like this need large flowers to give importance to the design. Pipe the flowers in advance. After the cake is decorated, begin the cascade. Use your eye to determine placement of the flowers. Start with clusters on tier tops, then fill in on cake sides to create a flowing cascade effect. Note that the flowers increase in size as they approach the base of the cake. Fill in with buds and leaves. The ornament is trimmed with tiny roses and leaves for a unified look.

THE CAKE IS CONSTRUCTED of three tiers, 14″ ×4″, 10″ × 4″ and 6″ × 3″. Upright tube 506 shells form columns around the base tier, with tube 506 shells piped on the side at the middle tier and tube 501 shells on the top tier. Garlands, scalloped detail and string drapes complete the decoration. This cake will serve 156 guests at a reception.

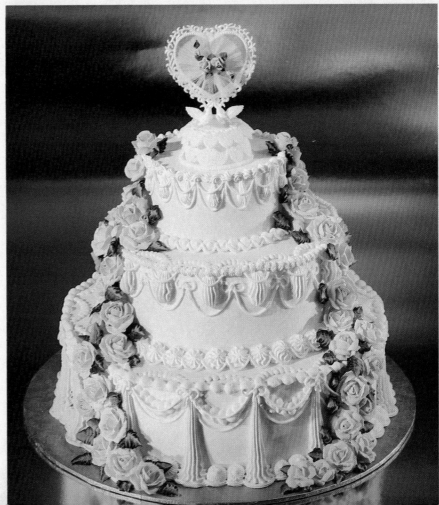

The Wilton School offers classes in all major decorating techniques

Since McKinley Wilton began teaching nearly a half-century ago, students have come to the famous Wilton School of Cake Decorating and Confectionary Art from every continent on earth.

Now more student applications than ever are being received and classes covering a great variety of decorating methods are made available to them. The three major courses are: *The Master Course, The Advanced Course* and the new *Lambeth Course.*

The Wilton-American method

The Master Course has for many years been attended by serious students, professional chefs, caterers, talented housewives and people who simply decorate for the sheer fun of it! They may come from thousands of points on the globe. All are taught to make scores of real-life flowers, to do perfectionist scrolls, garlands, and stringwork. During fifty closely

Cake decorated in the Master Course

Cake decorated in Advanced Course

Norman Wilton · commonsense for decorators

supervised hours they "paint in icing", discover new ways of using familiar tubes, design and decorate a variety of party cakes. Finally each assembles and decorates a wedding cake. On the tenth day, when diplomas are awarded, the decorating room looks like the site of a Grand Prix exhibition and the graduates are convinced the four hundred dollar tuition was money well spent!

Five foreign methods

The Advanced Course provides eighty hours of concentrated instruction in five foreign methods of decorating. Students work with *Mexican* gum paste, molding delicate flowers and charming party trims. They are introduced to *Philippine* flower making where royal icing blooms are piped on wires. They see first hand how "precision" takes on a new meaning when they move into the *English* method's *Nirvana.* They amaze themselves by turning out in icing the finely-detailed lace and intricate lattice that's the hallmark of the *South African* method. And they invariably are justly proud after creating an *Australian* method cake, embellished with dainty lace. Students receive a special Wilton diploma and a richly beribboned "Award of Excellence" medal on graduation day. The all-inclusive cost of the 10-day, 80-hour course is four hundred dollars, materials included. You'll participate in a *pulled sugar* demonstration.

Think lavish! Think Lambeth!

If you do, you'll want to enroll in the Wilton School's new ten-day, eighty-hour Lambeth Course. This English method is the one used to achieve many of the showpiece cakes of the past two centuries. So if you are looking for new challenges in decorating, you will be richly rewarded when you see the fruits of your labor. Instruction here is largely on a one-to-one, instructor-to-student basis and prospective students should have a good grounding in fundamental techniques. All materials are furnished. Cost of the Lambeth Course is four hundred dollars.

For further information write: Wilton School of Cake Decorating & Confectionary Art, 833 West 115th Street, Chicago, Illinois 60643.

How to design a tier cake— it's easy and fun

Many of you have asked this question, "How do you get ideas for cakes, especially wedding cakes?" I admit, planning a wedding cake is a little intimidating if you are not a very experienced decorator, but if you proceed in an orderly way, it's a very enjoyable task.

Determine the number of servings

Once you know how many guests are expected, consult the chart on page 159 for help in planning the size of the tiers. *Angel Celebration*, the cake at right, was made to serve 200 or more, so tiers were sized accordingly. Also determine if the top tier will be removed and frozen for the first anniversary.

Now sit down with a pencil and a piece of graph paper and sketch the cake in proportion. Let one square equal one inch. The height of two-layer wedding cake tiers is usually 4″ for the lower tiers and 3″ for the top tier. Be sure to include the pillars on your sketch. Decide on the top ornament at this time too. Rough it in on the graph paper. Often a petite ornament will be suitable for a very large cake. After you've finished the sketch, examine it to see if the proportions are pleasing.

A convenient rule

A good rule to follow is to have each tier 4″ larger than the one above it. For example, *Rosy Future* on page 21 has a 14″ base tier, a 10″ middle tier and a 6″ top tier.

This cake serves 156. If you need more servings, increase the size of each tier. 16″, 12″ and 8″ tiers will cut into 216 servings. Of course there are many exceptions to this rule of four.

Decide on the borders

Since a tier cake is usually large, the choice of border is very important. First choose a rather heavy and ornate border for the base of the largest tier. The other borders can be variations of it to give unity to the whole design. Leaf through books that show wedding cakes or borders and choose one to reproduce or vary as you like.

The base border on *Angel Celebration*, at right, starts with a simple shell. A heavy curved garland is draped over it, then strings are added. Shells are repeated on all tiers.

Large flower garlands on the middle tier repeat the curves, and the border on the top tier is a miniature of the one on the base. The lacy look of the pedestals for the angels is echoed in the top ornament. This cake is a very good example of unified design, and shows how simple it is to design a wedding cake.

Flowers add a grace note.

Flowers, of course, give you a good opportunity to introduce color, and are the loveliest decoration a cake can have. I recommend that the flowers be piped of royal icing. Then you can make them far in advance and mount some of them on wire stems for bouquets.

On the next page, you'll see how easily you can design party cakes.

Assembling a tier cake

To properly assemble a tier cake is an art in itself. Study diagram to see how each tier is supported by the one below it.

Add top tier

Insert dowel rods in tier same as for base tier

Place separator set on base tier

Push circle of dowel rods into tier to cake board. Clip off level with top. Separator plate will cover.

Read from bottom up. Each tier is set on a cake circle of same size.

How to decorate
Angel Celebration

1. Pipe many tube 33, 190 and 225 drop flowers with tube 2 centers. Bake the 6″ square, 12″ round and 16″ square tiers. Fill and ice, then assemble as the diagram shows. Use 5″ Corinthian pillars and 7″ square separator plates.

2. Always work from bottom to top when decorating a tier cake. Pipe tube 17 shells at base and top of 16″ tier. Divide each side of tier into sixths and drop a string guideline for the garlands. Pipe them with tube 17 and drape with tube 3 strings.

3. On middle tier, pipe tube 16 top and bottom borders. Divide tier into eighths and pipe a tube 16 string from point to point. Use this as a guide for attaching flowers in garlands, then pipe tube 3 bows.

Continued on page 158

Angel Celebration
Decorating directions at left

Norman Wilton · commonsense for decorators

DESIGNING A CAKE continued

4. Borders on top tier are the same as bottom tier, but tube 13 is used with tube 2 strings. Notice that as tiers get smaller, smaller tubes are used. Add tube 2 bow and flowers.

5. Glue a Winged Angel to the ornament and trim with flowers and ribbon. This gives the ornament individuality. Push Filigree Pedestals into the base tier and mass flowers around them. Trim all flowers with tube 65 leaves. Glue cherubs to pedestals. Tie a ribbon around the Cherub Fountain and set within pillars. Add more flowers. Angel Celebration serves 216.

A tier cake can inspire designs for many smaller cakes

This picture shows how Angel Celebration, page 157, led to the design of these party cakes. The New Year's cake in the background has the same decoration as the base tier of the wedding cake, but candles are used instead of cupids. The shower cake is almost a replica of the center tier and the baby shower cake repeats the top tier.

The importance of color

The warm orange and gold drop flowers on the New Year cake give a welcoming, cheerful effect. Peach and pink flowers against pink icing make the round cake very feminine. The baby cake is especially dainty with blue and green trim.

Novelties add interest

Well chosen plastic novelties can turn a simple cake into a real creation, tailored especially for the occasion. The clock face, parasol and bassinet give meaning to the cakes shown above. The angel figures on the wedding cake on page 157 add a note of festivity and joy. Always bring the novelty into the general scheme of decoration by trimming it with the flowers used on the cake.

Norman Wilton · commonsense for decorators

158

Batter and Baking Chart

All baking times are for preheated 350°F oven. For one-cake-mix shaped pans, follow baking instructions included with the pans.

Pan	Size	Cups of Batter	Baking Time in minutes
ROUND (2" deep)	6"	2½	25-35
	8"	4	30-40
	10"	6	30-40
	12"	9	30-40
	14"	11½	30-40
	16"	14	35-45
	18"	16	35-45
SQUARE (2" deep)	6"	3	25-35
	8"	4½	30-40
	10"	7	30-40
	12"	10½	30-40
	14"	13½	30-40
	16"	15½	35-45
	18"	18	35-45
PETAL (2" deep)	6"	2	25-35
	9"	4	30-40
	12"	6½	30-40
	15"	12	30-40
HEART (2" deep)	6"	2	25-35
	9"	4	30-40
	12"	8½	30-40
	15"	12	30-40

Pan	Size	Cups of Batter	Baking Time in minutes
HEXAGON (2" deep)	6"	1½	25-35
	9"	3½	30-40
	12"	7	30-40
	15"	12	30-40
RECTANGLE (2" deep)	9"x13"	8	30-40
	11"x15"	11	30-40
	12"x18"	15	30-40
LONG LOAF (4¼" deep)	16"x4"	12 (2 mixes)	55-65
LITTLE LOAFERS (1½" deep)	4⅜"x2½"	½ cup ea. pan	20-30
BALL PAN	6" diam.	2⅓ cups ea. pan half	35-45
BLOSSOM PANS	4⅝" diam.	¾ cup ea. pan	20-30
SMALL WONDER MOLDS (3" deep)	3½" diam.	¾ cup ea. mold	20-30

How to cut a wedding cake

To cut a tier cake, start by removing top tier. Then begin cutting second tier, third and fourth as shown. Remove each tier before cutting.

TO CUT ROUND TIERS, cut a circle 2" in from outer edge and cut 1" slices within it. Move in another 2", cut another circle and cut into 1" slices. Continue until each tier is cut. Center core can be sliced into two, four or more pieces.

TO CUT SQUARE TIERS, cut straight across side of tier, 2" in from outer edge. Slice into 1" pieces. Move in another 2" and slice this section into 1" pieces. Continue until entire tier is cut, then begin to cut the next tier.

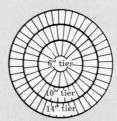

Top view of 3-tiered round cake.

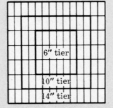

Top view of 3-tiered square cake.

CUT HEXAGON TIERS like round tiers.

CUT PETAL-SHAPED TIERS like round tiers.

DIVIDE HEART-SHAPED TIERS vertically. Slice 1" pieces within rows.

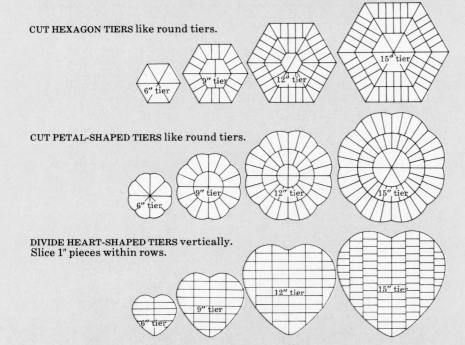

Party cake serving chart

Here is an approximation of the number of party-size servings you can expect from each size cake. One-mix cakes, of any shape, serve about twelve.

SHAPE	SIZE	SERVINGS
ROUND	6"	6
	8"	10
	10"	14
	12"	22
	14"	36
SQUARE	6"	8
	8"	12
	10"	20
	12"	36
	14"	42
RECTANGLE	9"x13"	24
	11"x15"	35
	12"x18"	54
HEART	6"	6
	9"	12
	12"	24
	15"	35
HEXAGON	6"	6
	9"	12
	12"	20
	15"	48
PETAL	6"	6
	8"	8
	12"	26
	15"	48

Wedding cake serving chart

When cut into 1" x 2" slices, this is the approximate number of servings from each tier.

SHAPE	SIZE	SERVINGS
ROUND	6"	16
	8"	30
	10"	48
	12"	68
	14"	92
	16"	118
	18"	148
SQUARE	6"	18
	8"	32
	10"	50
	12"	72
	14"	98
	16"	128
	18"	162
HEXAGON	6"	6
	9"	22
	12"	50
	15"	66
PETAL	6"	8
	9"	20
	12"	44
	15"	62
HEART	6"	12
	9"	28
	12"	48
	15"	90

Index